Sabine's War

Sabine's War

The Incredible True Story of a Resistance Fighter Who Survived Three Concentration Camps

EVA TAYLOR

Harper
North

HarperNorth
Windmill Green
24 Mount Street
Manchester M2 3NX

A division of
HarperCollins*Publishers*
1 London Bridge Street
London SE1 9GF

www.harpercollins.co.uk

HarperCollinsPublishers
Macken House
39/40 Mayor Street Upper
Dublin 1
D01 C9W8

First published by Hanover Square 2022
This edition published by HarperNorth in 2023

1 3 5 7 9 10 8 6 4 2

A catalogue record for this book
is available from the British Library

HB ISBN: 978-0-00-853088-4
PB ISBN: 978-0-00-851918-6

Printed and bound in Great Britain by
CPI Group (UK) Ltd, Croydon'

To Karen, Michael, James, Tjarda, Derk and Theta.

In memory of your Oma.

A drawing of Sabine Zuur by fellow prisoner Aat Breur in Ravensbrück concentration camp, Winter 1944.

Preface

When I visit my mother in the care home, she no longer has any idea who I am, but she is always delighted to see me. When I tell her I am her daughter, her face lights up, and she says, with wonder, "I did not know I had a daughter, but you are so lovely." She is by now in her early nineties, almost deaf and blind. Once every six weeks or so, I travel from England to Holland to visit her, and this short conversation is repeated endlessly during my visits. She is happy I am there, whoever I am.

She is settled in the home where she now lives and particularly enjoys the musical afternoons once a week. She always loved dancing, and in her confused state, it seems to be the only thing that she has not forgotten. As soon as the music starts, she jumps up and dances elegantly through the room with a happy smile on her face.

It reminds me of when we danced together when I was a child. During our evening meal, the radio often played nice music, and when she heard a favorite song, she would pull us out of our chairs to dance around together.

I often try and remind her of things in the past, but it's only when I go back a long way and talk about her brothers, who died decades ago, that she starts remembering. I sometimes ask her if she remembers the war and little bits come back to her. She tells them to me in a conspiratorial way, like a child who has been naughty.

Although she often talked about the war when I was young, it was always about food, about friends she lost, but never about life in the camps. This is probably because I never wanted to know about it, and perhaps she also could not bear to recall those memories. The horrors have no meaning when you are a child. But now, when it is too late, I am interested.

In her descent into Alzheimer's, she has become a loving, caring, kind person. A mother I suddenly love very much. Not at all the mother I knew as a child, and it made me realize how life's events really can shape you into a totally different person. I'd like to think that as her mind leaves this world, her personality seems to revert back to the child and young woman I have read so much about.

When she died in 2012, I found boxes and boxes of letters, photos and documents, mainly about her time in the war. I think I knew her well enough to appreciate that she hoped I would be interested in all this information. In enclosed notes, there were pleas not to just throw it all away.

Her story of the camps is similar to thousands of others, yet different. Some stories are well-documented, but for the many who died without leaving a trace, there are no stories to pass on. And those who found it too painful to tell their stories themselves are now often having them revealed through their children and grandchildren.

Sabine's story is but one very small piece in this horrendous period of history, but it is still important to pass it on to future generations, especially her own family.

It is only by reading through all her documentation that I begin to understand her peculiarities, and also discover the person she might have been if war had not intervened.

This is the story of Sabine's war.

The Hague

After the War

I grew up in a small second-floor flat in The Hague. I was four when my parents and I moved there, and my earliest memories are of playing in the ruins that surrounded our block of flats, an area heavily bombed towards the end of the war and not yet rebuilt in the early 1950s.

Other memories from that age are also vivid. Not long after we moved, I spent a long time in the hospital, and when I came home again, I remember I was suddenly presented with a younger brother, who appeared from seemingly nowhere. No one told children much about such matters in those days.

Life after the war was difficult for everyone. There was still not much food around, and I remember sweets and fruit were real treats. Winters were so cold my mother put horse blankets in front of the windows to keep the frost out. We had two small stoves in our flat, which were only lit if we had coal. It is hard to believe now that the coal man came once a week with a horse and cart carrying his deliveries of coal, wood and paraffin.

They were lean years just after the war. How lean I only realized once I had grown up myself.

I was always aware, though, even when young, that my mother seemed different from other mothers. She had no money, and yet she was always beautifully dressed and so glamorous. She seemed to have an indefinable aura. My friends, young as they were, were in awe of her. People seemed to go out of their way to help her.

But I also knew another side of my mother. One she never showed to the outside world. She often cried and spent most days in bed with the blankets over her head, leaving us in the care of her cleaner, Tante Cor, who came several times a week to help out (mostly unpaid, I later learned). Nighttime was obviously very difficult for my mother. Perhaps nightmares haunted her, as she usually only got up when everyone else went to bed, and then she would roam around the flat until the early hours, much to the annoyance of the downstairs neighbors, who would bang on their ceiling with a broomstick. But despite this sad side of her, there were plenty of girlfriends around, and she never lacked male attention. On evenings when she went out, she would be at her most glamorous, and no one would guess she had a care in the world. I loved seeing her dressed up and smelling her perfume.

She could be a loving and fun mum, but she could also suddenly burst into uncontrollable rages, tearing drawers out of their cabinets, throwing things around and punishing us for some minor misdemeanor. Her mood swings were a source of fear and mystery to us.

After years of starvation and an appalling diet, her digestive system was ruined and never really recovered. She was almost permanently ill with diarrhea and vomiting. Many types of food had a disastrous effect on her. And then there was the teeth-grinding when she slept. So bad and so loud we could hear it in the next room. Her already poor teeth, ruined in the war, eventually became little stumps. She hated it but could not stop doing it.

My father spent little time at home. He was always away for work and sometimes disappeared for weeks, leaving her without money or a contact address. When he was home, there was always a lot of arguing.

It was many years before I realized that these were all after-effects of the war, and that her recovery was not helped by the poverty that was also part of our daily life and the disaster that her marriage turned out to be.

From the Dutch East Indies to Holland

Sabine's life had started so promisingly. She was the fourth child and only daughter of Sabine Schlette and Louis Zuur, born in Semarang, Java, Indonesia, in 1918, rather as an afterthought.

Her brothers were seven, eleven, and twelve years older. Father Zuur was a bank director in Indonesia in the 1920s, providing the family with a very comfortable lifestyle. Sabine was spoiled and adored by the whole family, but in her early teens, she first became aware that life was not perfect.

Father, mother and Sabine had moved back to Holland in the early 1930s, but her three brothers, already grown up and independent, had stayed behind in Indonesia.

Just as the family had returned to Holland, her darling Pappa died quite suddenly when Sabine was around fourteen years old.

A few years later, her favorite brother, Joop, by all accounts a bit of a womanizer, also died suddenly and mysteriously, poisoned by a Javanese lover, it was rumored in the family.

My grandmother, also Sabine, but always referred to in the family as Moeder Bien, was left with a good pension. Initially life was very comfortable, but with inflation and the depression in the 1930s, plus the fact that Father Zuur had lost most of his money made in earlier years during the stock market crash of the Great Depression in 1929, his fixed pension dwindled to very little. The result was that mother and daughter were forced to move time and time again to ever smaller houses, causing Sabine to change schools many times. She struggled with the constant changes, but eventually they settled in The Hague, hopefully for good.

After school, though, life became fun again. Sabine had grown into a beautiful young woman, and had no ambition for further education once she left secondary school. And although she was very talented at drawing, her only wish was to become a secretary, marry a nice man, have children and live happily ever after.

Her cheerful, lively disposition, very attractive looks, good sense of humor, and above all, her love of partying, sailing, and having a good time, soon made her a popular addition to the social scene in The Hague.

Among her many friends were Erik Hazelhoff Roelfzema and Chris Krediet, who would both play an important role in the Dutch Resistance, and many others such as Gerard Vinkesteijn and Broer Moonen, who would ultimately pay with their lives for their bravery.

Taro

In my mother's archive, I found a bundle of letters, held together with a piece of string. In an accompanying note, there was an instruction: "Destroy after my death." I knew the letters were from Taro, her fiancé, who had been killed during the war and of whom she spoke often to my brother and me. She always kept in touch with his mother and two sisters even long after the war.

I hesitated for a long time weighing up whether to destroy the letters or read them, but in the end I could not make up my mind and put them back in the box.

Some years later, when I decided to record her life story, I came across them again, and my doubts resurfaced, but in the end I decided to read them to see if and what they could add to this story. She had, after all, not destroyed them herself. I took them out of the box and started to read.

When Taro and Sabine met around 1937, it was love at first sight. He admitted that, from the moment they met, she never left his thoughts again. Within a short time, they were inseparable.

Taro was a handsome young soldier, a second lieutenant with the Mounted Artillery in the Royal Army. His full name was Johan Willem Yoshitaro Roeper-Bosch. His parents were living in Japan at the time of his conception, hence his Japanese name, which means "lucky firstborn son."

Sabine at that time worked as a secretary at a small import/export company in The Hague. Her carefree life was full of fun, and being madly in love.

But dark clouds began to form over Europe. In September 1939, Germany invaded Poland, and Europe held its breath. In the autumn of 1939, Taro left his army base in Arnhem to start training as a pilot at the elementary flying school in West-Souburg, near Vlissingen in Zeeland, in the south of Holland.

A passionate and frequent correspondence, as well as regular visits to each other, kept them in touch. Some eighty-three letters from Taro dating from this period have survived.

And although they kept the intensity of their relationship quiet, they considered themselves engaged.

Both their mothers, however, objected to their relationship. I can only speculate as to Moeder Bien's uneasiness. Sabine was still living at home at the time and was rather careless with Taro's letters. Perhaps her mother was worried about the passionate contents. After all, Taro was a few years older and a man of the world.

I have no idea why Taro's mother objected, but she later became very fond of Sabine and cared for and supported her a great deal, during and after the war.

Taro was very bored in Zeeland. He had to study hard for his pilot's license, but there were few opportunities to practice

his flying, which had been the main reason he had decided
to become a pilot.

On October 23, 1939, during a rare flying session, his plane
crashed, wounding him and his copilot. They both escaped
with light injuries, but spent a short time in the hospital. A
few weeks later, they placed a notice in the local paper thanking all those who had been involved in their rescue.

Since Taro had been the higher-ranking officer, he was
held responsible for the crash and was accordingly sentenced
to ten days solitary confinement in the barracks, although the
sentence was not executed for several months.

At that time, rather than living on the base, he was lodging
with a local family. And after having taken Sabine to intro-
duce her to them, they took a great liking to her, encouraged
him to invite her as often as possible, and allowed her to stay
in his room—a very liberal attitude for those days.

While the threat of war came closer, their relationship became more and more serious, and there was much talk of getting married.

Taro even opened a bank account for her and deposited a
monthly allowance in it so that she could buy nicer clothes (he
felt she should not look like a shopgirl) and told her to look
for a small apartment, which could be their home when he
came to The Hague. Most importantly, it would mean they
would be away from Moeder Bien's prying eyes.

But despite the talk of wedding plans, Taro also had his
moments of indecision. He still wanted to see a lot more of
the world, and he felt that his salary was not enough to support them both. And although Sabine was perfect in his mind
and he worshipped her, she frequently fell off the pedestal he
put her on. He found it difficult to accept that she had faults,
and he began to have doubts when these appeared. He did
not like it that she was friendly with other men, she smoked

and drank too much, and most of all, she did not follow his "wise" advice. She also did not seem as obsessed with him as he was with her, and the fact that she did not reply to every one of his letters particularly annoyed and worried him. But perhaps her silences were a reminder to him that she did not like being told what to do.

She was having a good time in The Hague while he was studying hard. He often wrote to her twice a day, and while he sometimes admonished her in the first letter, by the second one he was full of apologies and adoration again. His doubts were always momentary.

As the threat of war intensified, the marriage plans became more serious. Perhaps the thought of marriage gave them an idea of stability in those worrying times. Taro even suggested that when war broke out, they should get married immediately as Sabine would then receive a widow's pension if he died.

The outbreak of the war drew threateningly close, and in his letter of May 8, 1940, he advised her to empty her bank account, convert all her cash into dollars, and keep them with her at all times in a small bag under her clothes. He also advised that as soon as hostilities started, she should go and stay with his mother, despite the fact that his mother had so far not been willing to receive Sabine.

"Just swallow your pride and contact her. Consider yourself her daughter. I will write to her that she must treat you as such."

He also worried that the planned visit on May 10 would be impossible because of increasing tensions of the fast-approaching war.

The plan for that weekend was that Jan van den Hoek, a mutual friend, would collect Sabine in The Hague in his car, and Sabine would drive them both to Zeeland. Taro was keen for her to practice her driving so that she would be mobile if chaos broke out after Germany invaded.

He was by now very busy with war preparations, and his ten-day punishment, which had only just begun, was terminated after a few days. It was a question of all-hands-on-deck.

For the first time, he was seriously worried that he would never see Sabine again. He wrote,

In case we never meet again, this is my farewell to you. All my love and care is for you, even if I cannot act on it. Let's hope we can meet again.

War did indeed break out, and the visit was obviously canceled, as on May 10, he wrote her a farewell letter, telling her she would always be in his thoughts and that he hoped that, if they never met again, she would have a happy life and would always love him as much as he loved her, although he of course hoped with all his heart that they would spend the rest of their lives together; he again urged her to "go to my mother, look after yourself and be sensible and for once take my advice," ending with,

Sabientje, it seems not possible that this is truly our farewell. We have to meet up again. I will long for you for the rest of my life. My deepest love, darling. Be brave and strong. I will always love you. God bless you.
Taro

Strangely enough, he made no mention of war having started.

This was Taro's last letter. Shortly afterwards, his flying school was evacuated to Northern France, and any further correspondence was impossible.

War

Although Holland was fully expecting war to break out, it was still a tremendous shock when, in the early morning of May 10, 1940, the first fighter planes appeared above Dutch soil and German soldiers crossed the border. They were the vanguard of things to come. Often dressed in fake Dutch army uniforms and helmets, they quickly conquered the bridges over the big rivers in order to facilitate the rapid invasion of the rest of the German army.

The fight only lasted a few days. On May 12, Princess Juliana and Prince Bernhard, together with their daughters, Beatrix and Irene, were evacuated by ship to England. Queen Wilhelmina and her cabinet followed a day later. On her instruction, the army was left in the command of General Winkelman.

After the terrible bombardment of Rotterdam on May 14, the destruction of most of Holland's air force, and the threat of Utrecht receiving the same treatment as Rotterdam, Holland capitulated.

The Dutch queen led her cabinet from London for the rest of the war, and the Germans were in charge in Holland.

I found a postcard in the archive that Sabine sent to one of her friends during this time. On it she mentions how scared everyone was by the continuous bombing during those first few days, which she both saw and heard.

Holland was immediately placed under military control, but by the end of the month, this was replaced by a new civilian government headed by the Austrian Nazi Arthur Seyss-Inquart, soon nicknamed "six and a quarter" on account of him being small and having a limp.

Initially the occupation did not seem to make much of a difference in everyday life, and there was optimism that this would be a short war. But slowly life did begin to change. Traveling around became difficult, food was getting scarcer, and freedom was generally curtailed.

It became clear that the Germans were there to stay, and Resistance efforts, especially by the communists, began to form immediately, but soon the rest of the population realized that their freedom and rights were in serious danger, and Resistance groups began to form everywhere.

Apart from those who joined the Resistance, there were many people who escaped or tried to escape overland via Sweden or Portugal, or direct to England by using boats, dinghies, canoes, in fact anything that would float. They fled in order to make contact with the exiled Dutch government in London and offer their services by either joining the Allied forces or becoming secret agents.

Some 1,700 courageous men and women managed to survive this hazardous escape route across the Channel, although many more tried and did not survive.

They were soon dubbed the *Engelandvaarders* (England voyagers).

Among those who arrived in July 1941 in London were Erik Hazelhoff Roelfzema and Peter Tazelaar. Erik had been a friend of Sabine since they were in their teens, and Peter she would only meet later during the war when they became involved in the same Resistance group.

Taro's Death

Immediately after the German invasion, all pilots and planes from Taro's air base were evacuated to France. As there were no up-to-date maps available, the instructions were to fly south following the Dutch, Belgian, and French coastlines to Berck-sur-Mer, roughly 50 km south of Boulogne. All other personnel from the base were advised to follow the planes as best as they could by car.

Taro's plane developed engine trouble at the Belgian/French border, and he was forced to make an emergency landing on a beach. Much to the bemusement of the locals, he decided to abandon his plane and hitchhike to Berck. Once there, he discovered that there was no spare plane for him, and therefore he was unable fly. He decided to instead make his own way to England via Paris. During his time in Paris, he worked for the Dutch military attaché organizing passage to England for Dutch army personnel stranded in Paris. He himself left for London at the beginning of 1941. As soon as he arrived, he managed to meet up with his old friends, Erik, Chris, and many others from Holland. He also met Peter Tazelaar.

In order to gain his full pilot's license, Taro decided to join the RAF, and after achieving this, he joined the 611 Squadron, which was based in Essex, and where he became quickly known as Ropey on account of his unpronounceable surname.

He flew many sorties along the French coast in Hurricanes and Spitfires, but during one of these, on October 21, 1941, his Spitfire was shot down near Berck-sur-Mer by a German Messerschmitt. He was twenty-six years old.

His family was only informed a month later.

The following letter from the RAF Missing Research and Enquiry Unit, British Forces, in France, formed in 1944, was passed on to Sabine via Taro's mother.

Sabine never mentioned when she received this letter, but it must have been sometime after the war.

During a map sweep I visited the Maire of Alette and was informed that a Spitfire, Squadron 611, crashed in the hamlet of Toutendal, Commune of Alette on 21-10-1941. Further investigation in the area at the scene of the crash revealed that the aircraft was seen in aerial combat and was finally shot down in flames, the pilot being killed instantly and badly burned. The airman's body was eventually recovered, having no head or legs and almost all clothing was burned from the body. Nevertheless, an identity disc was found and the Maire of Alette took a copy of the inscription "J.W.Y. Roeper-Bosch. Off. 89295 R.A.F.V.R."

The wife of the Maire herself placed the body in a coffin provided by the Germans. She stated that the coffin was of a very extravagant type. The Germans then took the body away in the direction of Berck-sur-Mer.

It was a devastating blow for Sabine. She never recorded her feelings of that time, but I know it had an enormous impact on her. For the rest of her life, she talked about Taro and always stayed in contact with his family. I have even been named after one of his sisters. We children knew him as someone very special.

The Resistance

My mother often talked about the war, especially the hunger and cold she suffered. We were never allowed to leave so much as a spoonful of spare food on our plates. Every scrap was carefully kept. And yet she spoke very little about her Resistance work, or her years in the camps. There were just fragments of stories, which, as a child or even a grown-up, did not give me a clear insight into what had happened.

I was therefore not only surprised but also thrilled and intrigued to find her very detailed archive. I had never known of its existence. Apart from the already mentioned letters, it also contained letters from friends, identity papers, some with unknown names, some blank. I wonder if they were for some of the people who were in hiding with her. There was even an envelope addressed to Prince Bernhard, but no letter within.

As the German restrictions made everyday life more and more difficult, resistance and sabotage became a preoccupation for many who were left behind.

Sabine had an extensive and close-knit circle of friends, most of whom seemed determined to become involved with the Resistance, as was Sabine herself. Like many others, she was strongly opposed to the ideals of the German Reich, and when an opportunity presented itself, most likely through Gerard and Broer, to join the Resistance herself, she took it with both hands.

The first national Resistance group, formed mainly by retired and serving military officers, but also many civilians, was the *Ordedienst* (OD). It was an organization whose aim was to keep public order within the population should chaos break out when the Germans left. They could take charge during the vacuum created between the Germans leaving and the Dutch government and army returning. Obviously, everyone still had high hopes that this would be not too far in the future, and the *Ordedienst* wished to be prepared. The country was divided into nineteen areas, each with its own commander in charge, in case of unrest. When it became clear that the German occupation could last some time, they concentrated their efforts on sabotage, espionage, and funding and helping people in hiding.

From the *Ordedienst* sprang many small independent local Resistance groups, including the one that Adrien (Broer) Moonen, a police inspector in The Hague, and Gerard Vinkesteijn, an architect, and ultimately Sabine belonged to. Broer was so called because he had four sisters and, as Sabine said, "He was like a brother to all of us." Others who were part of this group were Eva (Taro's sister), Chris Krediet, and his father, Dr. Krediet. The whole group were friends from long before the war. Peter Tazelaar also came into contact with this group when he returned from England on his secret mission.

Sabine became involved at the beginning of the war, and one of her first tasks was to find safe addresses for people needing a hiding place. She took them there herself, but also started using her own house for those needing to stay some-where out of the public eye.

Friends and strangers came and went, for shorter or lon-ger periods. Peter Tazelaar stayed a month with her in 1941. Cosmo Medici (Bill) Roeske, another Resistance man who had tried to flee to England and failed, stayed for two months. Even some English pilots shot down over Holland found their way to her. She also acted as a lookout during meetings.

It was very dangerous work, and although the less one knew of what was going on the better in case of arrest, Sabine of course got to know most of what was being organized. At one time she even found a secret transmitter tucked behind her desk. She had no idea who put it there, and it disappeared as mysteriously as it had appeared.

How dangerous the work was became apparent when two Dutch policemen, Poos and Slagter, both working in The Hague for the *Sicherheitsdienst* (the Security Service of the *Schutzstaffel* paramilitary organization [the SS], which would later become one of the most feared and powerful organi-zations in Nazi Germany), were searching for some people Sabine was hiding. These two were subordinates of Broer Moonen and obviously did not realize his part in the Resis-tance. Because of his work, Broer was very much aware of what they were up to and any other potential actions by the SD (*Sicherheitsdienst*), and was therefore invaluable to the Re-sistance groups in The Hague.

He warned Sabine to be extra-vigilant, but Sabine, like many others involved, did not seem to realize the extreme danger her actions exposed her to. Everyone was still con-vinced the war would soon end and would be won.

Peter Tazelaar

For a long time, I thought that my parents only met after the war, but by reading my father's biography a few years ago, I learned that they first met at the beginning. I gathered that Peter was instantly smitten with Sabine. Whether she felt the same way, I do not know. At Christmas in 1941, Broer Moonen organized a dinner at his parent's house. He had invited the whole Resistance group, including Peter. Peter did not want to go, but since Sabine was going, he agreed to go too. To his disappointment, she only had eyes for Gerard Vinkesteijn and, upset and jealous, Peter left halfway through the dinner.

After Peter's secret arrival in Holland towards the end of 1941, he needed a safe place to hide. Sabine first organized a short stay for him with Taro's mother, after which he came to stay in her house for a month. Due to his departure for England and her imprisonment in Germany, they had no further contact until after the war, when they met up again and within a short time got married.

Like Sabine, Peter was born (1920) and brought up in the Dutch East Indies, with his younger brother, Jan, by his mother, Helena, a schoolteacher, and a very strict and over-bearing father, Jan.

Peter, even as a child, was a free spirit, always breaking the rules. By the time he was eighteen, he spent his time drinking, partying and chasing girls. His parents despaired. Whatever career they suggested, Peter was not interested. Then his father suggested the navy, in the hope that they would teach him some discipline.

At last, Peter was thrilled. He envisaged an exciting life at sea, but discovered very quickly, to his immense disappointment, that he would be land-based for the first year or two and be learning drills and theory and discipline.

This did not appeal to him at all, and after the first disastrous year, by mutual agreement it was decided that he was better off finding a different career.

In 1939 he went to live with his uncle in the north of Holland and joined the maritime school there. Shortly afterwards, war broke out, and Peter immediately determined he was going help fight against the invaders.

He tried several times to reach England but was unsuccessful, so instead he joined the newly formed *Ordedienst* and started carrying out assignments for them in the form of intelligence-gathering and sabotage. But before too long, by June 1941, he was on the German radar and was advised by the *Ordedienst* to stop his activities. The danger to himself and the others in his group had become too serious.

Instead, the head of the *Ordedienst* sent him on a new mission: to make his way to England and make contact with the British Secret Service to ask for help and support for the Resistance the *Ordedienst* was organizing.

Peter decided to look for a job at a shipyard in Rotterdam and soon discovered a Swiss ship, the *St. Cergue*, which was flying under a Panamanian flag and was waiting to be released to ship grain to the United States. Peter got himself a job on board as a maintenance man.

The *St. Cergue* was finally ready to depart on June 30, and after some problems with the existing crew being too drunk to sail, Peter was taken on as crew. Another young man, equally keen to get to England by any means, had also found a place as a crew member. This turned out to be Sabine's childhood friend, Erik Hazelhoff Roelfzema. As soon as the harbor was left behind, the ship turned north towards Iceland, and before too long, a third young man was found on board, as a stowaway, Bob van der Stok. Both Erik and Bob were students. Peter was the "Indonesian boy with a gold necklace," as Erik described him later.

Nearing Norway, a patrolling British cruiser insisted on inspecting the cargo, and the three young men decided to take their chance and asked to be transferred to the cruiser, which would take them England. The captain of the *St. Cergue* was not pleased to lose his crew, but agreed to let them go.

After having been deposited in the Faroe Islands, the three men made their way via Scotland to London, where they arrived at the end of July 1941. They immediately made their presence known to the Dutch authorities, who interrogated them for a few days and then let them go, despite their offers of help. Peter was itching to get back to Holland and play an active role in the Resistance. But the Dutch government was not impressed by the constant stream of *Engelandvaarders* turning up and demanding action. Queen Wilhelmina, by contrast, was delighted and insisted on meeting all those who made it across the Channel personally.

Seeing no prospect of any action by the Dutch authorities, Erik and Bob devised their own plan to set up contact between England and Holland, involving a wet suit, a dinner suit, a top hat, a dinghy and a bottle of brandy.

Bob left after some disagreements, and Chris Krediet, another *Engelandvaarder*, took his place in this madcap scheme. It was some time before the plan was approved, but in the autumn of 1941, under the guidance of Colonel Euan Rabagliati, a British colonel attached to the Dutch section of the British Secret Service, better known as MI6, it was finally put into action.

The plan was to set up a communication system with the Resistance in Holland to find out where and how they were operating. The organization fell to Erik and Chris. Peter would be the secret agent who would be dropped off in Holland.

This was a role he was very suited to: action, adventure and danger. The operation would be called "Contact Holland." The plan would be to cross the Channel by motor gun boat (MGB) and drop off Peter, as hopefully the first of many secret agents, on the beach near The Hague. His task would be to set up a network of agents and radio operators.

Several attempts to cross were launched and failed due to bad weather and engine trouble, but eventually, on the night of November 23, 1941, they managed to reach the Dutch coast around 11 p.m. The MGB dropped anchor some distance from the coast, and Erik and Chris rowed Peter towards the shore until they were fifty meters out. There Peter and Erik, both wearing wet suits, slid overboard into the sea and waded towards the beach in temperatures of −20°C.

The promenade of Scheveningen, a seaside resort of The Hague, was forbidden territory between the hours of 6 p.m. and 8 a.m. German headquarters were based in the Palace Hotel there, and the Germans feared an invasion aimed at that part of the coast. It was therefore heavily patrolled. It had been decided that Peter, should he run into a German patrol, would pretend to be a drunken student oblivious of the curfew. A not unnatural role for him.

As soon as they reached the beach, Erik quickly helped Peter out of his wet suit, to reveal a dinner suit including a bow tie, a top hat and black shoes. A bottle of cognac appeared from Erik's pocket and was sprinkled over Peter while they both took some large mouthfuls to fortify themselves after the icy trip and drown the fear of what lay ahead. Erik returned to the boat, and Peter turned into an almost legless student, lost after a party.

After a short walk across the beach and the promenade, he made it safely to the big square just behind the Kurhaus Hotel, where he took the first tram passing and made his way to the house of Dr. Krediet. While paying on the tram, he realized by the reaction of the inspector that there was something wrong with his money. Unbeknownst to London, the Germans had changed the coins from silver to a cheaper metal. The old money was out of circulation. Luckily the inspector pretended not to notice.

Her Majesty's
Courier

While in Holland, Peter not only had to fulfill his intended task of setting up a network of radio operators and secret agents, but shortly before his departure, he alone had been informed that Queen Wilhelmina had personally requested to have two men of her choosing brought back to England by the same route, and she wanted Peter to approach them. Men she thought would be useful to her war cabinet because of their knowledge and awareness of the situation in Holland. During his training for the landing, he was given a third task. So top secret even his friends in this operation were not allowed to be told.

He was to find and set up an escape route for RAF pilots shot down over Holland.

As Sabine was helping some of these pilots and even hiding some of them in her own home, it was natural that Peter and she would meet. Besides, all Peter's new friends in London and the contacts he would make in The Hague were already her friends.

Once Erik and Chris dropped Peter off at the beach, Peter made his way to the house of Dr. Krediet, father of Chris, in Wassenaar. Doctor or Dokkie Krediet was delighted to hear that not only that his son had safely arrived in England, but also that he was involved in this particular operation.

Dr. Krediet himself was very involved with the Resistance and in particular with the group that involved Gerard Vinke-steijn, Broer Moonen and Sabine. He played a very useful part. Being a doctor meant he was allowed a telephone and was also allowed out after curfew, which meant that he could not only visit patients but also transport equipment and any-one needing a safe house. Like the others, he would later be arrested and sent to Dachau Concentration Camp, where he died of typhoid.

When Peter arrived at Dr. Krediet's house that evening, he found not only Gerard and Broer there but also Sabine. She organized his first safe house, which was with Mrs. Roeper-Bosch, Taro's mother, although he later came to stay with Sa-bine for a month.

He was not the only one who came to stay. Many people who needed a hiding place passed through Sabine's house for shorter or longer periods. She looked after them, cooked for them and passed on messages. Her hospitality was gratefully received, and some of them, including some English pilots, stayed lifelong friends.

But apart from her job and her Resistance work, there was still time for parties and sailing, and on the surface, life car-ried on as normal.

Meanwhile, Peter's first task, setting up a network of op-erators, was soon in progress.

His second task, approaching the two men the queen had requested to be brought to England, was less successful. Wiardi Beckman, known as Stuuf, a left-wing politician and editor of an illegal newspaper, readily agreed to take the dangerous risk of departing in a small boat from the beach under the nose of the Germans. The other man, Captain Tielens, a high-ranking military man and chief of staff, refused to go. He had given his word of honor to the Germans that he would not work against them and refused to break his word. Not even for the queen and the exceptional circumstances.

During his short time in The Hague, Peter had met up with his old friend Gerard Dogger from his marine days, who was in desperate need to disappear. The Germans were hot on his tail for his illegal activities. Peter decided to offer Tielens's place in the boat to Gerard instead.

For his third task, Wiardi Beckman and Gerard Vinkesteijn offered some useful contacts. At Peter's request, Gerard decided to try out an overland escape route for English pilots that they had plotted together.

As he left on January 6, 1942, Gerard sent a short note to Sabine:

Dear Sabientje,
I have decided quite suddenly to go on holiday for a fortnight, so I won't see you for a while.
I received such a nice invitation and decided to accept it immediately.
Lieve knulletje, I have to go now. I will probably not be gone longer than a month.
Much love from your Gerard.
Remember, don't gossip.
Bye, sweetheart.

Three days later, Gerard was arrested on the train between Antwerp and Brussels. He would be executed in July the following year.

Failure and Disaster

My father never considered himself a hero. As a child I heard others mention him as a hero, and I asked him, "Daddy, are you a hero?"

He looked surprised and said, "No. Absolutely not. The real heroes are the Frisians who helped me at the end of the war. I didn't do anything special." (The Frisians lived in northern Holland, where Peter executed another secret mission at the end of the war.)

He was always very reticent about his war exploits with us as well as with any journalists, and mostly refused to speak about his experiences.

But because he is so much part of the story Erik Hazelhoff Roelfzema wrote about in his book *Soldier of Orange*, I slowly came to know his own story as well. It was impressive enough for him to be awarded the *Militaire Willems-Orde* (the highest decoration of the Netherlands) in 1944, as well as the *Bronzen Leeuw* and the King's Medal for Courage. Both Peter and

Sabine received the *Verzetsherdenkingskruis* (Resistance Remembrance Cross).

They both felt an obvious duty to help their country and were willing to risk their lives in the process.

Several attempts were made by Peter to meet up with Erik for their return trip to England, after the prearranged signal from Radio Orange, the Dutch broadcasting service in London, came to nothing.

Peter decided to try one last time, and that evening, Sabine arranged a dinner at her home for Peter, Gerard, and Wiardi Beckman as well as Frans Goedhart, a journalist and late addition to the group, who was also desperate to flee Holland. They were all to accompany Peter on this dangerous mission. A fifth man, Wim (Padje) Pasdeloup, would also accompany them to the beach to receive the transmitters that Erik was bringing. It would be their last meal as free men.

Later that night, Peter and Gerard, in their usual dinner suits (still a cover in case of arrest) and including top hats, lay on the frozen pier head, while Wiardi Beckman, Frans Goedhart and Pasdeloup sheltered in a nearby bunker. All were waiting for Erik's boat.

Unfortunately, the men in the bunker were discovered by a passing German patrol and were instantly arrested. Wiardi Beckman was sent to Dachau, where he died. Goedhart was sentenced to death, but in the end survived the war. Pasdeloup succumbed to the mental and physical torture he was subjected to and broke and named names. To silence him, he was eventually murdered by his own Resistance partners.

Peter and Gerard, although a bit further away, were clearly visible in their dark suits against the frost and were very fortunate that the patrol did not search the surroundings any further. In a great panic, Gerard pulled Peter into the icy sea. They had already lain on the frozen pier head for several hours, and now they stood for some time in deathly silence up to their necks in the −20°C sea. Peter soon became semiconscious through hypothermia. Gerard managed to drag him further down the coast to another part of the beach, where they finally dared to crawl out and make their way to a nearby safe house, where they were revived by a bottle of jenever.

The day after this debacle, Peter received another signal via Radio Orange to tell him an MGB would pick them up that evening. London did not as yet know about the disaster of the night before.

Peter felt responsible for Erik, who after all was also about to risk his life for him, and decided, despite strong reservations, that he and Gerard would go to the beach again. After the previous night, the Germans had realized something was going on and had increased security patrols. Unfortunately, before Peter and Gerard even got to the beach, they ran into a German patrol. In their by now dilapidated-looking evening dress, they looked like third-rate waiters, and even their drunken behavior did not fool the Germans. Luckily, Peter managed to drop his pistol in the snow before being dragged off for questioning. As soon as they entered the German police station, they were confronted with a wanted poster of Gerard on the wall.

Peter had the presence of mind to start behaving so appallingly drunk that the Germans' interest focused on him, and they did not realize that the wanted man was sitting in front of them. Within a few minutes, Broer Moonen, the police inspector and their friend, walked in by chance and immediately realized what was going on. Exclaiming that he had been looking for these two drunkards, he explained he had been accompanying them home and they had escaped, but now that they had been found again, he would make sure that this time they got home safely. Because he was a respected inspector and their superior, the Germans agreed to release these two idiots into his care. It was a very lucky escape.

Peter and Gerard urgently needed to leave Holland as they were now both on the wanted list since Peter was linked to the failed plan of the night before. By the time of Peter's return to Holland at the end of 1941, the Germans had become suspicious of the *Ordedienst*. They suspected this Resistance group was behind the murder of a German officer and, as a result, they had arrested the head of the OD. Peter had also been a member of the OD, as was Gerard Dogger, Peter's old naval mate, who was suspected of being complicit in this murder. This was why Gerard was already being hunted by the Germans. When he and Peter were caught trying to return to England, the Germans did not realize that by letting the two men go, Gerard had slipped through their fingers, although when they did, Peter was immediately also suspected. The Germans' information most likely came from someone within the OD. Because of this, further attempts at landings and setting up networks had to be abandoned. Plan Contact Holland had been compromised.

Broer Moonen put Peter and Gerard in contact with a group who organized escape routes to England via Belgium, France, Switzerland and Portugal and who helped them to escape Holland. He was a true friend in need and deed.

Not long afterwards, on February 27, 1942, Broer Moonen himself was betrayed and arrested. He too would be executed.

Betrayal and Arrest

Sabine had been warned. On April 15, 1943, Gerard Vinke-steijn's sister, Isabel, sent Sabine a letter from her brother, smuggled out of the Utrecht jail where he was awaiting his sentence. In an accompanying note, she wrote, "The poor man carries his burden courageously."

Gerard's letter was written on both sides of two cigarette papers no bigger than 4 cm by 7 cm each, in miniscule hand-writing.

With much effort and the help of a magnifying glass, I eventually managed to decipher the contents, seven hundred words in all.

Gerard wrote that he had been interrogated thoroughly about a little notebook that Sabine had sent him. Although he was punished severely, he stayed silent. He also brought up the subject of Sabine's boss, who I will refer to here by the name "Piet." Piet apparently was bragging about his work with the Resistance to anyone who would listen. "My opinion is that

Piet is a bad Dutchman, who profits from the enemy. I hope
I am wrong, but I doubt it."

He also instructed her what to do in case she was arrested:

> I think you are already well known. Perhaps they are
> not looking for you, but try and be invisible. If you have
> to, you can admit that Peter visited you with a message
> from Taro and that you suspected that I did some illegal
> things, but you did not know why some people visited
> you, and [you] therefore objected to further visits. What
> Bill (Roeske) has said about you I do not know, but it is
> known that he stayed with you and that there was a trans-
> mitter in your house. Bill has given a lot of information
> about you, but you have to keep denying that you knew
> anything about the transmitter or what Bill was up to.
> As far as I know there is no danger of you being arrested.

Bill was Cosmo Medici Roeske, who had spent two months
in hiding with Sabine. While trying to escape to England, he
was arrested, interrogated and executed. Somehow Gerard
had found out that Bill had told the Germans about Sabine.

Gerard already knew by this time that he would be executed
and asked Sabine to please keep writing to him:

> I am allowed to receive limitless parcels and letters—
> I hope to receive many more letters with your cheer-
> ful gossip. I count on three or four more weeks in this
> world, so please hurry. I am also allowed photos. Broer
> will give them back to you later.

But Broer had by now also been arrested and was also awaiting execution. Gerard had no illusions about his own chances
even though the legal process was still ongoing. He wrote,

This morning sentences have been announced. Death for the first 25. Tomorrow the appeals. Darling, I already know the decision and I am proud of it. Don't idolize me, you know how difficult I can be. Keep your memories of me realistic.

Right at the bottom, he scribbles, "Lots of kisses G."

Sabine should have been on her guard for her boss, Piet, when she arrived at work on the morning of April 28, 1943, and spotted a military car parked near her office. It was strange and worrying, but she soon forgot all about it. Inside all was calm and normal. Her boss usually arrived later in the morning. But that morning, within half an hour of her arrival, he phoned her, and they had a short conversation about nothing in particular. That was also strange, as normally he never phoned to check on her. But within minutes, the doorbell rang, and two men, one Dutch, one German, wearing raincoats and hats, came in and arrested her.

They escorted her to the waiting military vehicle that she had seen earlier and drove her back to her flat. Once there, the men turned her flat upside down, but, disappointingly for them, did not find anything of interest until they emptied her handbag and found her address book. Instantly they decided to take her in for questioning. She was instructed to put the address book back in her bag and take it with her. The men politely offered to lock her door when leaving, but Sabine asked them if they could first put her rather large potted plant on the landing so her neighbor could water it while she was away. To her surprise, they agreed, and while they were carrying the plant outside, she quickly hid her address book behind a cushion on the sofa.

Her interrogation in the infamous interrogation rooms at the Binnenhof, in the center of The Hague, did not take long. After a few hours of threats and much shouting, she was transported to Amsterdam.

Amsterdam—Utrecht-Amersfoort
Polizeigefängnis Amsterdam

The Wednesday that Sabine was arrested was a cold but sunny day. It would be a long time before she would see sunshine again.

Her first stop was the *Polizeigefängnis*, a police prison on the Amstelveenseweg in Amsterdam, where she would stay in between interrogations at the feared headquarters of the *Sicherheitsdienst* (the Security Service of the SS) on the Euterpe Street.

There, in between interrogations, some of them lasting hours, she would have to wait in a small, dark cell downstairs for her next turn. The cell contained only a straw mattress on the floor, and a small barred window high up provided the only light. There was nothing to do but listen to the rattle of the cell keys, the slamming of doors and the screams of the guards and prisoners alike. During the first "interview," she was forced to admit she had no idea what had happened to her address book. On the whole, women were treated less harshly than men, but her silence infuriated the Germans, and they beat her several times, but she kept repeating she knew

no names and otherwise stayed silent, despite new interrogations and beatings every few days.

The feelings of fear and oppression never left her, with the
constant anticipation of the door being wrenched open and
being dragged out for yet another interrogation upstairs. The
dread of what they might already know and of what they
might do to get information out of her made her very scared.
On top of that, boredom breeds anxiety, and there was plenty
of boredom. She could not shake off the fear of the unknown,
the insecurity.

At the end of each interrogation day, she was returned to
cell D-27 in the jail on the Amstelveenseweg. The regime
there was harsh. Her single cell, when she arrived, already
contained six other women.

Letters to
Moeder Bien

In my mother's archive, I found quite a few small bits of paper, scribbled letters, which she wrote to her mother from both Amsterdam and Utrecht jail.

Apart from these pencil-written but still surprisingly readable scraps, I also found a few "official" letters to her mother. She was allowed to write these once a fortnight, but they had to be "businesslike."

The smuggled letters give a good insight into the close bond between mother and daughter. Sabine always tried to stay positive and not worry her mother. She inquired after friends, encouraged her mother to stay positive, and even wrote about the progress of the war, of which a surprising amount filtered through into the jail. After Moeder Bien had had no news of her daughter since her arrest in April, she finally received her first official letter from Sabine, dated June 11, 1943:

Dearest Mams,
I am so happy that I am allowed to send a postcard home

to ask for a parcel of food. It may weigh up to 2 kg, but
nothing in tins or glass. Please send something like sugar
or jam etc. You are also allowed to enclose a letter to
me, max twenty words. I hope all is well with you. I
am very well! Hopefully see you soon. A big hug from
your Bientje.

Regards to you and Eva and all my friends.

From time to time, Sabine was allowed to receive food parcels and clothes. Once a week, she was allowed to send and
receive her laundry, which Moeder Bien had to collect and
bring in person. Official letters were allowed once every two
weeks. I found only three of them in her archive. Her second
official letter relates to her mother's gold watch that she happened to wear on the day of her arrest. She wanted her mother
to collect it together with most of the money she had on her,
although "I will keep some of it for my train journey home."

In her third official letter, she asked Moeder Bien to bring
her dark blue shoes with rubber soles, which were better for
floor-cleaning duties that had now been assigned to her. Although Sabine's carefree life had so far not included scrub-
bing floors, it was clearly better than doing nothing all day.

While the official letters were only allowed once a fortnight, Sabine soon found a way to exchange secret letters with
her mother. The most obvious route lay in the weekly laundry.
Although all laundry was carefully inspected, they nevertheless found places to hide the letters. All seams were searched,
but apparently not pleats in skirts. Sabine was always surprised
that the guards were not suspicious of the same purple skirt
going in and out with the laundry every week.

Her method was simple. By wrapping her letter, written
on a cigarette paper, around a whalebone stay from one of her
cellmates' corsets, she managed to insert the scraps of paper
into the top of the pleat. When these papers ran out, she asked

her mother to wrap her laundry in tissue paper, thus giving her a new supply. "But please, Mams, rub the paper for your letters between your fingers to soften it, so that it doesn't make a noise."

Moeder Bien also hid small pencils in the corrugated bottom of the specially provided laundry bag. In the beginning, they enclosed a small red comb each way to indicate that there was a hidden letter, but Sabine feared that it would be too obvious. She worked out a different system using the label that was part of each laundry bag indicating the clothes in it and also any food items that Moeder Bien had added, with sometimes a brief note: "Kisses from mother" (I found quite a few of these in her archive).

Sabine instructed her mother carefully:

On the label mark the item with a letter with a Z. If I return a letter I will mark it with an X.

In this way, quite a few letters went to and fro. Often there were requests for particular clothes or toiletries, but also information regarding the state of the war and news of friends and relatives. Small things could also be included in the laundry, "but nothing valuable. The chance of it being stolen is great." She even suggested small things could be hidden in her sanitary napkins, "as I don't think the male guards will take these apart."

In every letter, she assured her mother that she was well and not unhappy. She was managing well. But she also said she had been interrogated several times again, and each day brought the worry of yet another one. She seems to have been beaten regularly.

But despite all this, she was also very worried about losing her apartment and asked her mother to keep paying the rent from her salary, which she hoped her boss was still paying her. She was getting very homesick by now, but made sure her mother did not suspect this. On the whole, her letters were positive and cheerful.

In her first smuggled letter, she asked after dear Gerard, who by now had been in prison for some time. She also asked her mother to warn her boss, Piet.

May 18, 1943
Dearest Mams,
I have already been interrogated twice and fear it will happen many more times. Awful. Warn Piet (in connection with Jan van den Hoek). He is known to them. I have only passed on Piet's telephone number to Jan in connection with "something" that he wanted to send abroad. Otherwise I don't know anything. Now they are beginning with a third interrogation about Gerard etc. Mams, please write to me how they all are. Find out from his brother. I really hope they make it to the end of the war. Do you think it will end soon? We are aware of what is happening in the outside world. All is well with me. We are now six in our cell again. Luckily the smelly one is gone.

Now a few things I would like to receive with the laundry on 28th May: a small pencil (hide it), something sweet, but cheap. A good chance it will be stolen. Also hair grips, sunlight soap (ask Cees), toilet soap (ask Ton) and Nutrogen cream (ask Carolien). Lots of love and kisses. Sabine

Jan van den Hoek was the ex-boyfriend of Eva, Taro's sister. He was the friend with whom she would have driven to see Taro on the day war broke out. He was also active in the

Resistance and was arrested a few days after Sabine. He had managed to get hold of maps showing the German reinforcements around the mouth of the River Maas, and he wanted to pass on this valuable information to "someone abroad."

He had asked for Sabine's help, because she was in contact with Peter Tazelaar as well as English pilots. Unfortunately, most of her friends in her Resistance group had by now been arrested. The reason she asked Piet was that he also had his own connections abroad, having studied at the Sorbonne. After the war, she declared that she always thought Piet was unreliable because he was such a liar, but that he seemed to have no political interests. Jan's name was mentioned several times during her interrogations, and she was afraid that the link to Piet would be discovered. Despite his apparent neutrality, she slowly but surely found out that Piet had in fact played quite a different role.

Even though all laundry was carefully inspected, there were some two hundred laundry baskets going in and out of the prison, so the chance of the letters being discovered was relatively small. She was still worried, though, about the address book she hid in her sofa when she was arrested.

Dearest Mams,
Finally. I received some laundry. Poor you. I can so imagine how horrible all this is for you, but, don't worry, I will get through all this. The war cannot last longer than this winter, don't you think? The laundry control is now very thorough, so I will hide my letters in four different places. Make sure you look everywhere and let me know if you have found them. I am desperate to hear from you. Did you receive my apartment keys? Keep everything locked up and please remove my notebook

(on the brown sofa) and Gerard's album from my desk.
I hope you have eaten my butter?

In this letter, she again advised her mother to warn Piet,
because she was very worried he would also be arrested. The
tone of this letter was more somber than usual due to the recent
interrogations, which were "horrible" and "nerve-wracking."
Her cell was revolting. On top of that, she was still very worried about Gerard and Broer:

Mams, contact Gerard's brother to ask how Gerard is.
And tell me honestly, even if it is bad news. I need to
know. I can't sleep at night thinking about them. Please
tell me. Promise me you will be careful? Some people
have been here for months for trifling things.
   Oh yes, Mams, do not hand in my radio. Tell them
it has nothing to do with you. It is my business and not
yours. What can they do to me. I am already here.
   And another thing: you will have to go and ask for
my ration card in the Euterpestraat, room 42. Don't go
yourself, but send someone who supposedly does not
know me and cannot give any information about me.

These instructions might have been worrying, but the following paragraph might have made her smile.

Order biscuits every week, on my behalf, at the bakery in
the Bachmanstraat, then save half of them for me. Buy as
many as they will sell you. I will refund you the money
or coupons later. When I get home I will eat them all
in one go. I feel happy just thinking about it. I am sali-
vating already when I think of a cheese bun or a custard
pudding. Let alone a rijsttafel in Tampat Senang.

The Tampat Senang was a famous Indonesian restaurant in The Hague.

> June 16, 1943
> Dearest Mams,
> A big thank you for the delicious Whitsun parcel. I am so delighted with it. Please phone Eva Roeper-Bosch. She was also jailed here in Amsterdam, but was found innocent. When is it my turn? I will surely be here till the end of the war.

That same morning, a large transport of women was sent to Vught and Ommen camps.

> At least they have fresh air there. I won't be going anywhere as long as they want to interrogate me. Write to me about Gerard!

At the end of June, her mother visited the jail to collect the keys to Sabine's apartment. They had hoped to see each other, but it was not allowed. Sabine was desolate: "Mams, I cried and cried when you came for the keys. I had to show them which ones and when I asked if I could see you, he bit my head off. Back upstairs I cried and cried, you see, there are days when life feels so oppressive and I want to crawl up the wall, because I want to feel free again. But on the whole things are bearable."

It is clear that Sabine struggled to keep up her morale. Hearing news from her mother both cheered her and at the same time depressed her.

On July 15, it was Sabine's twenty-fifth birthday, and her mother sent her a surprise: "Mams, I am so happy with the

beautiful bouquet of flowers and when I saw your card with
birthday wishes I burst out in tears."

She again asked for news of Gerard and whether her mother
had warned Piet yet. "You know, sometimes it is so difficult
to keep going, especially now it is summer and the weather
is so nice."

Fortunately, her situation suddenly improved somewhat.
A Dutch doctor, who was working as a volunteer in the jail,
asked her to assist him looking after sick prisoners. She was
moved from her overcrowded cell to the sick prisoners' cell,
which was much bigger and cleaner. Best of all, the food was
much better. The prisoners slept on small iron cots, and Sabine slept on a straw mattress on the floor.

About her new cellmates she wrote:

I am now in a cell with a German Blitzmädel [part of the
female branch of the Hitler youth], who is very sweet.
She has had a miscarriage and had a nervous breakdown
due to having been at the Front. Her husband is Austrian.
She offended a general who fancied her.

No. 2 is a married woman of thirty-seven, very sweet,
sometimes irritatingly so. She suffers from panic attacks
and gallstones. They are especially awful. The other day
she was sick twenty times. She helped Jews.

No. 3 has been here for seven and a half months.
She has a very swollen knee due to a fall and is thin as
a broomstick. She is suspected of being a communist.

The three women even took the trouble to write to Moeder
Bien to tell her how well Sabine was looking after them.

The Blitzmädel wrote in fractured Dutch:

Dear Madame. I hope I may call you that. Thank you
very much for the excellent care of your daughter. We

are all prisoners and we must all help each other as much
as we can. She is very brave and looks after us very well.
Bye, dear Madame. I may be German, but I love it here.
Christel

About No. 2, Sabine wrote underneath: "And now another
victim. Daag."
No. 2 wrote:

Dear Madame. We are very fond of Sabine, she looks
after us like a proper nurse and the cell is sparkling clean.
She is a good child and we hope for you that she will
soon go home. Helma

At last No. 3 got her chance: the suspected communist.

Madame. Sabine has nursed me very well. You can be
proud of a daughter like her. The only thing is she ruins
the floor cloths too often. She wrings them out too force-
fully. Greetings from her cellmate. Lies Vreeken

This nice arrangement unfortunately did not last long. On
July 27, Sabine wrote:

My luxury job has finished. A German nurse has replaced me and I am now back in a cell where there are
four cases of scurvy. But don't worry about the dirty
laundry. It is so hot in the cell, we are all sitting around
in our underwear.

More and more items were now stolen from her parcels. Sabine had asked for some needles, and Moeder Bien had hidden
these in some meatballs. "I received my parcel Friday night,
but without a label. When I asked about it, I was shouted at.

From your letter I understood that a lot of things were stolen from it. The meatballs were missing. I hope they choked on the needles."

Moeder Bien also sent her some good news regarding Gerard. "I am so glad Gerard is still alive. I am hopeful for him again. He has already been in jail for nineteen months, the poor man. And I for three months, although it seems like a year."

On a separate bit of paper added to the same letter of July 27, she wrote:

> Darling Mams. We all expect to be home before 1st October. We are expecting the invasion any day now. If I am freed, I will come straight home, so do not come to Amsterdam. Stay at home, lieverd, promise me. There are no longer any transports to Germany. Book a hair appointment now already for me at Legrand for around that time. Bye, lieverd. Your excited S

She could not know that Gerard had only two more days to live. He would be executed on July 29, 1943.

Sabine never forgot to thank her mother and her friends for all the food and other things that they sent her, although much of it was stolen before it could reach her.

Her letter of August 10 started with a long list of food that had been stolen by the guards. She was also fed up with her cellmates. "I am now sharing with four women all older than forty and very pious. They are all new here, some of them have only been here two weeks. Boring."

But there was something more important in her letter. She had heard that sixteen men had been executed, and she had hoped that her mother would pass their names on to her.

Why didn't you? I am sure that Gerard and Broer were among them and I am heartbroken. Some of them were architects and policemen I heard.

None of the new prisoners, from whom this news must have come, could remember Gerard's or Broer's name on the list.

Therefore I am a little hopeful again they were not among them, but, please, Mother, do not leave me in this terrible uncertainty. If they were on it, tell me. You should have done so already, because now I have to wait for another fortnight again, till the next letter. I also need to know with regard to the next interrogation. It could make a difference in my declarations. Think about it (but do not mention it in your letter).

She also wanted to hear news of two recently married couples whom Moeder Bien knew.

I am so jealous of their happiness. Why am I so unfortunate in my love life. First Taro and now Gerard, who, even if he survives till the end of the war, I will never marry. But don't think for one moment that I regret anything, Mams. On the contrary. But the war has ruined so much for me, just as it has for thousands of others. Without the war I would have been happily married and been a mother by now, enfin, it is what it is. But I can't help dwelling on these thoughts sometimes. Dearest Mams, I miss you so much and also all my dear friends. Bye, darling, lots of kisses and love from Sabientje

★ ★ ★

On August 12, there was a short note. Sabine had found out herself that Gerard was executed.

> Dearest Mams,
> You don't need to write to me about Gerard any more.
> I just saw the list with the sixteen names. I hope Gerard
> is now happy. The worst is over for him, only…so near
> victory. Tell me everything now! In haste, S

Gerard had been executed on July 29, aged thirty-six. Sabine's heart was broken. Apart from her sadness, for the first time she became seriously frightened of what might be waiting for her. Until that moment, she had been telling herself that she had committed no crime and that she would be freed at any moment. But Gerard's execution changed that. She had, after all, worked closely with him. Would the same fate await her?

Among all the documents, letters and laundry labels, I also found something quite different: the farewell letter from Gerard to his mother.

After the war, Gerard's mother sent Sabine a copy of this letter, written in the *Kriegswehrmachtgefängnis* (an armed forces prison run by the German military) in Utrecht, a few hours before his execution. It is a moving letter, and I hope it gave his mother some comfort.

> My dearest and courageous little mother,
> Yes, here I am, feeling radiant. Happier than I have been
> in all my thirty-six years. In my personal feelings there is
> only one shadow over my extreme happiness, caused by
> a deeply felt sense of compassion and pity for you, who
> are forced to take part in my happiness. Moedertje, this
> afternoon at two thirty this shadow will lift, because the
> good God has agreed to receive this thirty-six-year-old

person of little consequence. It is an eternal example of
His goodness to be content with one so unimportant and
to say: come to me, my child. And dearest Mother, I feel
so ashamed towards you, who has already lived a much
longer and more difficult life and who has not yet been
able to receive this ultimate happiness. [...]

I enclose a hair lock.

There are some more pious sentences, but he ends by saying,

And now, Mother, having looked deep in your beautiful eyes I ask you to forgive me for the sadness and many
worries I have given you. After thirty-six years you have
won. In the end you are the loveliest woman, my great-
est love. I know this will help you. You cry now and I
understand that my darling. I have no more tears, my
happiness is complete. [...]

Darling, a long and heartfelt kiss from your own, and
so proud of you.
Gerard. So long

This letter must also have been heartrending for Sabine,
even though she would only read it years later. The relationship between Gerard and her must have been very close. Again
she had lost a dear friend and possibly lover, due to the war.

Sabine originally thought she had been arrested because
Gerard and Broer had been arrested some time before her,
and she wondered if the *Sicherheitsdienst* had made the connection between them. But slowly it also began to occur to
her that her arrest might have had something to do with her
boss. He had been unconcerned when her mother tried to
warn him, at Sabine's insistence. Might his telephone call at
her office have had something to do with her arrest? Had

he informed the men outside that she had arrived at her office? She now seriously wondered if he had betrayed not only her, but others too. After the war, her suspicions were proven to be true.

After Gerard and Broer had been arrested, Sabine contacted all their mutual friends to collect food for them and put it all in a suitcase and rucksack. When wondering who she could ask to take this to them, her boss, Piet, offered to go in person. On the agreed day, a mutual friend had run into Piet at the station and, knowing about the food delivery, asked him where the rucksack and case were. Piet told him he had put them in the luggage depot for the moment, although everyone knew that these were unlocked and everything deposited there was immediately stolen. Gerard later confirmed he never received the food.

Piet himself was also arrested during the war while on a train carrying smuggled guns, and via Camp Vught ended up in the Sachsenhausen Concentration Camp, where he was freed by the Russians. Immediately after the war, when he returned to Holland, he was arrested again, this time by the Dutch authorities. It appeared that he had been working as an informer with the Germans as well as the Dutch, earning large amounts of money for his information in the process. He confessed after the war that he had passed on the names of Jan van den Hoek, as well as those of Gerard Vinkesteijn, Broer Moonen, and "Sabientje 'Suur'" to a German contact, who, to all intents and purposes, pretended to be a member of the French Resistance. He spent two years in jail but was released due to lack of evidence. Sabine was the only one from her Resistance group to survive.

Kriegswehrmachtgefängnis Utrecht

Sabine spent four months in the Amsterdam jail, but on August 25, she was manacled to a male prisoner and transferred to the *Kriegswehrmachtgefängnis* on Gans Street in Utrecht to be sentenced.

Among her papers, I found an official-looking card with a small hole in the top. The tear along the top indicates it had hung on a nail, but otherwise it is in good condition. The information on it is as follows: Zuur, Sabine Louise; DOB 15.7.1918; her prison number, 1101; and her offense: *Spionage und Feindbegünstigung* [spying and helping the enemy].

The accompanying note instructs me not to throw it away and explains it is the identity card that hung in her prison cell in Utrecht.

Only at the beginning of September did Moeder Bien receive some news from her daughter, her one fortnightly letter she was allowed to write.

The letter heading bears the stamp of the Kriegswehrmachtgefängnis Utrecht. Next to it is Sabine's name and number: 1101.

What a shame that you came to Amsterdam for nothing, as I had already left for Utrecht on the 25th August. I have meanwhile received your laundry and the food parcel. Thank you so much!

Here I may receive a parcel and laundry every week and also cigarettes and flowers. I am looking forward to those! I can also receive unlimited letters. Please ask everyone to write to me. I would like to have your photo that is on my desk too. And, Mams, please ask to speak to the commandant and ask if you can visit me. It will probably be allowed and it would be so lovely!

In a smuggled letter written the following day, on September 6, eight pages long, Moeder Bien finally found out what had happened the previous week.

On August 25, for no reason indicated to Sabine, she was suddenly, after four months' incarceration in the Amsterdam jail, transferred by train, under armed guard, to the *Wehrmacht* jail in Utrecht to be sentenced. On this public and humiliating journey, she was accompanied by five guards and another four male prisoners, one of whom was manacled to Sabine. It was the first time in months that Sabine was out in the fresh air and seeing people going about their daily business. She had no idea what was going to happen to her. "Mams, I was so scared, I thought the end had come."

The sentencing two days later took place in a big cold hall decorated by a large *Hakenkreuz* (swastika) flag. Of the other four suspects, she knew only Jan van den Hoek. His name had been mentioned several times during her interrogations.

In her letter of September 6, she wrote:

Present 27th August at 9 a.m., spoke briefly to our "lawyer." The five of us were made to stand in front of a big green table: the Kriegsgerecht [court martial], consisting of five high-ranking German officers. Apart from our lawyer and us there was a translator and our interrogator from the Sicherheitsdienst.

The officers stopped for a lunch break between 1 and 2 p.m. She did not record if the prisoners got any lunch or were just made to wait. The verdict was given the same afternoon.

I and two others were "abgetrennt" [forced labor until the end of the war] and Jan and the other man were sentenced to death. There will be an appeal of course. There is 80 percent chance of a pardon apparently. Hopefully I will not be sent to Germany, although there is always a chance.

Sabine's conviction was *Feindbegünstigung und Spionage*. Later she was rather proud of that label. Compared to Jan, she got off lightly. In passing, on the way out, she tried to say some encouraging words to Jan and the other man, but what can one say to a condemned man? Jan, who had been arrested a few days after Sabine, was executed in secret three weeks later on September 18, 1943.

Sabine also fell in the feared *Nacht und Nebel* category, meaning no one was allowed to know where she was or even if she was still alive. If she died, no one would ever know. She would disappear without a trace.

Compared to the jail in Amsterdam, living conditions here were considerably better. The German commandant of the jail turned out to be a "gentleman," according to Sabine. "He allows the cell doors to be open during the day and we can socialize and eat together in the two big cells. We are allowed to receive unlimited cigarettes and parcels and we are allowed to wear makeup."

About her fellow prisoners she wrote:

This is a nice jail. Sixteen women. I share a big cell with three others. There are also two Belgian women here. They, as well as two others, have been sentenced to death. But women always are pardoned, according to the commandant. I am accused of "Behilfe zur Spionage." Most of them are here for similar reasons and most have a husband or fiancé who is or will be condemned to death. Terrible. Luckily we are allowed to sit outside in the courtyard during nice weather. Once a week a warm bath. What a luxury jail, Mams…we are very optimistic here and think the war will be finished before the end of the winter, especially since it looks so promising in Italy.

Hopefully we will meet soon again. Bye, lieverd. Lots of kisses. Bientje.

In the summer months, the Allies had landed in Italy, and at the end of July, Mussolini had been arrested and deposed. A few days before Sabine wrote her letter, on September 3, 1943, after weeks of negotiations, a truce had been signed between the Allies and the Italian government. The good news spread far and wide, even into the jails.

The women's quarters where Sabine was housed were separate from the main building. They had their own courtyard and entrance. Meals were taken in one of the large communal cells, around a large wooden table.

The SS guards were cruel, though, and the commandant, knowing this, assigned some Dutch female guards to his female prisoners. They had stayed on from when the place was an ordinary jail before the war. He knew they would be kind to the women, as indeed they were. One of them, Miss Toll or Tolletje, was too kind and was herself sent to Ravensbrück, where she met up with Sabine again, but also where she died. They made life bearable for the prisoners. Drawing materials were brought in for Sabine, and a local women's group was allowed to bring extra toiletries and food. One of these women was Grace Steijns, the wife of Sabine's doctor. The couple were both gynecologists in Utrecht and also involved in the Resistance. Michel (Chel) Steijns was arrested himself not long after Sabine was in Utrecht. He was sent first to Camp Vught, and later to Mauthausen, where, by some miracle, he and Sabine met up again.

Towards the end of September, Sabine wrote another letter to her mother thanking her for the beautiful flowers. One of the friendly guards had told Sabine that when Moeder Bien delivered the flowers to the jail, she had been rudely treated by the guard at the entrance.

> Mams, don't worry when the German guard at the entrance shouts at you. Sometimes the guards come in here and shout at us, but the fat Dutch female guard says not to worry. They are Wehrmacht and harmless unlike the SS guards, like the ones we had in Amsterdam, who are bastards.

She apologized that she constantly asked her mother for more food, but her cellmates always shared their food with her, and she wanted to reciprocate. The meatballs her mother sent her, even though made of surrogate meat, were much appreciated by all.

> The trousers you sent are lovely and warm, but I am putting on so much weight around my hips. All my clothes are too tight. Everyone is putting on weight, due to lack of exercise and too much food. As soon as I get home, it will all go. Are you looking after yourself and are you eating enough? Are you managing to keep going?

By now, Sabine had learned that Broer Moonen had also been executed, about a week after Gerard on August 7, 1943. She wrote to her mother:

Poor Broer. I was so looking forward to at least see him again. He was Gerard's best friend and always supported him loyally. Now they also share the same fate. I always hoped Broer could explain a lot of things to me about their arrest and sentence etc. I hope there is someone left from their cellmates who can tell me these things.

The morning of his execution, Broer sent a farewell letter to his father and four sisters.

"Dearest sisters and father," he wrote, "this morning I have suddenly been told that I will be executed at 2 p.m. I will die without fear and with my head held high." His execution took place near Amersfoort, the same place where Gerard's life ended too. He was twenty-nine years old.

Since all Sabine's fellow prisoners were accused of similar serious crimes and no one had been sent to a concentration camp for a while, she was hopeful that she would not be sent either. In a smuggled letter a few days later, she again thanked her mother for the food she sent. Everything, the cake, the cheese, was delicious.

But what was even better was the encouraging war news. According to rumors in the prison, the battle between Russia and Italy was going well.

Thanks to all the letters from her mother and her friends, she was up-to-date with the latest gossip from home. News of impending births inspired her to make little cloth animals to send to new babies. She asked for needles, bits of material and stuffing to be added to the next food parcel. The toy animals she made never reached her friends. Before she could send them, she was moved. After she left the Utrecht jail, Moeder Bien collected them along with her clothes and the identity card that hung in her cell, and which she had secretly sewn into her clothes to keep as a souvenir. Stealing documentation was a serious offense.

I have always kept the little animals, and I am still amazed that my mother made these. As far as I knew, she could hardly sew on a button.

By now, mother and daughter had not seen each other for more than five months. On October 8, 1943, Moeder Bien received a telegram that must have caused her great anxiety:

Phone between 6 and 7 to number Utrecht 19516. Urgent.

When Moeder Bien phoned, she was told that her daughter would "go on transport" the following day. Sabine hoped that, while she was taken from the jail to the car, there would be an opportunity for them to see each other in passing.

Very upsetting, but tomorrow I will be sent to a camp, probably Vught. I really liked it here and have been busy making little rabbits for all the expected babies. [...] From the fact that the two others who were abgetrennt [sentenced to forced labor] are also leaving tomorrow and the two condemned men are not, I understand that the punishment has already been completed. Poor boys. Another two, Jan van den Hoek I knew, but not the other one. He was engaged. Enfin, all this feels very unreal at the moment, but once I am home, I will realize it all much better. When will that be? Oh God, dearest Mams, if only you knew how much I long to be home. So mean that [if] you did not get permission to visit me, it will probably not be possible in a camp either. But I hope we can see each other tomorrow, even if it is at a distance. I hope it will not make you too sad, but I am sure you will want to see me too.

I am being sent, as the only woman, together with thirty-seven men and of course the necessary guards. I have been given lots of food and hopefully, wherever I am, I will still be allowed to receive parcels. So for the moment I have plenty to eat.

I have no idea if Moeder Bien was able to go to Utrecht, and if she did, were they able to see each other? It seems unlikely.

Meanwhile, the Russian army was making good progress and recaptured several cities. The news from the Front was a shot in the arm for the prisoners. They were so encouraged by it that several women had already packed their suitcases, ready to go home. Sabine too, was very optimistic.

"Mams, the war is going fantastic, isn't it? There is still a chance I will be home for Christmas." She ends with, "Bye, darling Mams, keep faith. I will be home soon, really. Lots of love and a big hug. Sabine."

Altogether Sabine had spent nearly six months in Amsterdam and Utrecht jails.

Polizeiliches Durchgangslager
Amersfoort

After having been informed brusquely by the commandant in Utrecht that she would be leaving the following day, she as the only woman in the company of thirty-seven men found herself once again chained to a male prisoner and loaded into the back of one of two trucks that were sealed off at the back with a heavy tarpaulin. No one could see in or out of the trucks. Inside it was pitch-black. Surprisingly, Sabine had been handed back her fur coat as well as her makeup bag for the journey.

She later said, "While we were being loaded up, two of the men were very polite and introduced themselves to me."

Instead of going to Vught, as she had expected, she was taken to Amersfoort Concentration Camp. A male camp only.

Polizeiliches Durchgangslager Amersfoort was a police transit camp and officially a holding place for prisoners who were to be sent east. In practice it was also a labor camp where mainly political prisoners and Resistance people were kept. By the time Sabine arrived there, the camp held a few thousand male prisoners. The camp commandant, Karl Peter Berg, would be

sentenced to death after the war. His assistant was the feared
Josef Kotalla. He became one of the infamous Breda Three, the
last German war criminals who were held in Dutch jails after
the war and would be sentenced to life imprisonment.

Sabine's observation of him: he was a small man, and you
could see he bit his nails. During her imprisonment there, he
interrogated her twice.

Although a few other women passed through the camp
from time to time, Sabine's arrival created a great disturbance.
The commandant was very displeased to see her. Since she
was the only woman in the camp and could not be placed in
the barracks with the men, the only option remaining was
the punishment bunker. This was a concrete building with
small, dark cells where the prisoners were kept. Sabine ended
up in Cell 18.

Camp Amersfoort consisted of two parts. On one side stood
the barracks for the prisoners, surrounded by very high barbed
wire fences and watchtowers. This area was only accessible
via the SS camp next to it. Here the SS guards were accom-
modated as well as the camp administration. Sabine's bunker
was situated in this area. Her guards were young Dutch SS
men. When one of them entered her cell, wearing a too-big
helmet and uniform, he looked so much like a child that Sabine asked him how old he was. "Seventeen," he said. When
she asked him if his parents were happy that he worked there,
he admitted that they were angry with him. Although as soon
as he realized what he had said, he got very cross and beat
her. His fury was probably more with himself than with her.

The guards continually spied on her through a gap in the
door, giving her no privacy at all. If she wanted to change her
clothes, she had to turn her back to the door so they could
not see her. Her small, dark cell contained only a narrow cot
and a dirty bucket in the corner.

A few days later, while walking through the corridor to collect her daily bucket of water, she heard a guard shouting at a prisoner and, after a short silence, a shot. She was so shocked, she dropped her bucket and ran towards the cell to see a German soldier standing over a prisoner who had fallen on his knees, begging for mercy. The poor man had had no food or drink for the last three days and had not been allowed to relieve himself during that time either. He was pleading to do a pee. Sabine was so incensed that, without thinking of the possible consequences, she went up to the guard and pushed his hand holding the gun away. The guard was so surprised, he forgot to shoot her. A lucky escape for her. It could have turned out very differently.

Among my mother's papers, I found a pile of official-looking documents (in German) relating to a hearing that took place in the camp. I spotted Sabine's name on it several times, but it took quite a while before I managed to understand what took place during the first few days after her arrival and what these papers had to do with her.

Her arrival had caused not only great consternation but also a great upheaval within the camp itself. As a result, three Dutch SS guards would be dismissed and transferred to other camps.

On Monday, October 11, two days after her arrival, an SS officer reported that the *Lageralteste* (a Dutch prisoner who mediated between the Germans and other prisoners) had approached him to say that the prisoner Frans van den Berg, who worked as a chef in the camp, had spent time in Sabine's bunker. This had been allowed by the three Dutch SS guards, the *Blockführers*, Westerhuis, Appelo and Gombert. The *Lageralteste* also added that *Blockführer* Westerhuis had smuggled cigarettes into her cell. The *Blockführers* were in charge of the barracks. These three often had guard duty in the bunker, which always had extra security because it was a punishment bunker. A day later, chef Frans van den Berg was called to account. He admitted that he had indeed visited Sabine and had asked her why she was there. Sabine had told him that many of her friends had been executed, but that she had no knowledge why and therefore did not understand why she was imprisoned. "That is all we spoke about," declared van den Berg, "although I admit I sat next to her on the bed while we chatted."

Frans van den Berg had been imprisoned in Amersfoort since it was built in 1941 and had been a chef from the start. He was considered the most powerful prisoner in the camp, because he had the freedom to move throughout the camp and therefore was able to pass on any news of what was happening anywhere in the camp. He had been head chef in a restaurant in The Hague before the war and was arrested after making some anti-German remarks during a speech. It was a major mistake. It would cost him four years of imprisonment in Amersfoort.

On Sunday night, van den Berg had visited Sabine for half an hour in her cell. The night before, when Sabine had arrived, van den Berg together with *Blockführer* Westerhuis had also visited Sabine in her cell to bring her evening meal.

Chef van den Berg declared, "Since Saturday evening I have been able to speak several times to Sabine in her cell. The Blockführer did not interrupt."

You might think van den Berg perhaps also had other ideas in mind, and this tallies with what *Blockführer* Gombert declared during his questioning: "I knew that the prisoner (v.d. Berg) had visited Zuur several times and he told me that 'mit dem mädel nichts zu machen sei' [nothing doing with this woman]." In other words, the chef had made advances towards Sabine, but she had managed to ward him off.

The interrogator asked Gombert if he did not know she was a *Nacht und Nebel* prisoner and was therefore not allowed any contact with the outside world. Gombert admitted that he knew this.

The whole affair was considered very serious. It is likely that Camp Commandant Berg himself was present throughout the hearing, and he certainly signed off on the papers himself.

From a separate hearing regarding another *Nacht und Nebel* prisoner, it is evident that other prisoners, on the initiative of *Blockführer* Westerhuis, collected cigarettes and even a bottle of cologne for Sabine.

As a result of this upheaval, the three *Blockführers* were taken into custody and dismissed. Gombert and Appelo were sent to Camp Vught. What happened to Westerhuis is not clear, although he too was dismissed. The chef stayed in Camp Amersfoort until it was liberated by the Canadians and even then stayed on for some months longer to cook for the prisoners too ill to be able to leave the camp.

In 1995, my daughter Karen, for a work project regarding the fiftieth anniversary of liberation, when interviewing her grandmother, was told stories of which I knew nothing. Some of these have been of great interest for this book. One of them concerned Camp Amersfoort.

"At nighttimes a guard would walk up and down the corridor to check on the prisoners, but one night I heard him approaching very softly and stopping outside my door. I was very afraid he had come to rape me and curled in the farthest corner of my bed, clutching all my clothes against me to protect myself. But he came in very quietly and kneeled by my bed and whispered, 'Listen. Three men are planning to escape, and they want you to come with them. They will wait for a moonless night. I will leave your door unlocked that night. Go to the office, where I will leave the key to the outside door on the desk. Then walk to the barbed wire fence at the end of the yard and wait there.'"

It was a badly thought-out and reckless plan. Although the bunker stood outside the main area, from the watchtower, which stood exactly in the middle between the SS side of the camp and the prisoners' side, any fleeing prisoner would be clearly visible.

When Sabine came to the camp, this news of the arrival of a lone woman had spread like wildfire. Everyone was convinced she would be executed. When she received news of the escape, she had an impossible decision to make. She herself also expected to be shot, and therefore there was nothing to lose in trying to escape and possibly die in the attempt. Equally she still hoped she would be allowed to go home, and she did not want to jeopardize her chances of release. It was an agonizing decision: go or stay. The outcome might be the same.

On the evening before the escape, the number of guards was suddenly increased, and a loud banging on her door announced the arrival of Commandant Berg and his assistant, Kotalla. Sabine was in the process of mending her overcoat when the men entered. Her bucket was turned upside down, her cell was searched, her mattress was torn open, and Commandant Berg ripped her coat out of her hands and shredded it. ("I later repaired it again," Sabine said defiantly.) Berg and Kotalla were clearly looking for something, probably a letter that had supposedly been smuggled into her cell. They were furious. No incriminating evidence was found to indicate that she was part of an escape plan.

Sabine never discovered whether the men planning the escape were found out or who they were or indeed if there ever really was an escape plan.

Moeder Bien had not heard anything from her daughter for several weeks and was very worried. She decided to send a letter to the court in Utrecht seeking information regarding the whereabouts of her daughter.

The *Kriegsgericht* returned a short note to her:

> Regarding your request of 19th October 1943 we hereby inform you that according to a decision taken in this case stl.1n1 107/43 no information can be given.

After three weeks in Camp Amersfoort as the only female, she suddenly heard women's voices. Another nine women had arrived in her cell block. They turned out to be her old cellmates from Utrecht.

The following morning, all the women were put on a train to Haftanstalt Kleve, a correction house just over the border near Kleve, Germany.

They stayed there for a few days before they were transported in coal wagons to their final destination.

On the way, the women discussed what might be waiting for them: Where were they going? For how long? In any case, they concluded, it could not possibly be worse than Amersfoort. At least they would not be shut up in a dark damp cell.

"We were so naive," Sabine said later.

On the way, they stopped at a station that was being bombed as they passed. Everyone was told to leave the train. Sabine contemplated escaping, but sense prevailed. Where could she go? Who in Germany would help an escaped Dutch prisoner?

"But if I had known what was waiting for me," she said years later, "I would have taken the risk and run."

The journey ended at concentration camp Ravensbrück, about 80 km north of Berlin, where she arrived on Monday, November 1, 1943.

Another awful chapter was about to begin.

Ravensbrück

Frauen-KZ Ravensbrück

On the rare occasions that my mother talked about her time in the camps, she would more often mention Ravensbrück than Mauthausen. But then, she spent nearly a year and a half in Ravensbrück and only a few weeks in Mauthausen.

On the whole, though, she actually said very little in detail about the long eighteen months she spent in the women's camp, apart from mentioning the cold and the hunger. There is no personal documentation, either, unlike from her time in the jails in Holland and in Mauthausen.

However, I know a lot more about her time in Mauthausen thanks to the letters I found in her archive.

For a reconstruction of her time in Ravensbrück, I was therefore dependent on reports from eyewitnesses and general literature about the camp. In the 1980s, Sabine was contacted by Dunya Breur, whose mother, Aat, was a prisoner in Ravensbrück at the same time as Sabine. Dunya came to interview my mother several times regarding her own time there and related many of her and other victims' stories in her impressive book *A Hidden Memory*, a memoir of her own mother's time in

Ravensbrück. I feel sure that through her research, she began to understand her mother as I have begun to understand mine.

By reading Dunya's book and, indeed, many others, I gained a good impression of what Sabine's time in the camps was like. Sabine herself also wrote several reports after the war for the Red Cross and Stichting 1940–45, an organization set up to support those who had suffered and or lost loved ones during the war. After I had finished sorting through her archive and I finally put together a picture of what happened to her, I decided I would like to visit Ravensbrück and see for myself what the camp had been like. My brother, Peter, accompanied me as we drove from The Hague to Ravensbrück.

In some ways, the camp proved a surprise. Hardly anything of the original camp structure is left. It now is a very large, mainly open area. All that is left to see are a couple of the old barracks as well as the contours of the original barracks, which are still visible on the ground. One of the barracks is now used as a museum, and another one is used for storage. The surrounding wall is still there too. It is hard to imagine the dirt, the noise and the fear that inhabited the camp in those far-off days.

Camp Ravensbrück is situated some 80 km north of Berlin. In 1938 and 1939, German male prisoners from nearby Sachsenhausen Concentration Camp were moved to Ravensbrück to cut down trees and level the ground in the sandy marshland area and build first their own barracks and then accommodation for the thousands of female prisoners expected to arrive over the coming months and years. It was the first and sole concentration camp for women only.

The provincial town of Fürstenburg, in the province of Mecklenburg, is situated on one side of a beautiful and calm lake, the Schwedtsee, and the horror that was Camp Ravensbrück lies directly on the opposite side of the lake. It is a very quiet and peaceful area with plenty of lakes and dense forests of pine trees. This part of former East Germany now boasts many spa resorts, is popular with walkers and cyclists, and is ideal for boating holidays. The only reminder of the war is the notorious name of Ravensbrück.

In the six years of its existence, more than 130,000 women and children were kept prisoner there.

Although the camp originally was built for around 3,000 prisoners, in 1942 it already held 15,000 prisoners, and in 1944 as many as 70,000. Sabine guessed the number at 40,000 when she arrived.

Tens of thousands died. The precise total is impossible to calculate because the Germans destroyed a great deal of their administration just before the end of the war, but the guesstimate is around 28,000. All died due to slave labor, starvation, poisoning, torture, exhaustion, injuries and illnesses, executions, medical experiments and the general barbaric conditions in the camp. Many went mad.

Towards the end of the war, male prisoners were forced to build extra gas chambers where between 5,000 and 6,000 women were murdered in the last few months of the war.

The camp was originally built to house political prisoners. Communists, Resistance fighters and political activists from more than forty countries arrived over the years, particularly many from France and Poland. Some 2,000 Dutch women were also incarcerated there.

Trains carrying women and children from all over Europe arrived at the little station in Fürstenburg, where they were met by yelling guards with sticks and machine guns, accompanied by barking, growling dogs. The women were forced to run the few kilometers to the camp (uphill), some still carrying their suitcases.

Once there, everything was taken away from them, including glasses, false teeth, hearing aids, walking sticks, and medication, and often even their hair was shaved off. They were made to undress, and all body openings were searched. After this first humiliation, the women were paraded naked in front of sneering German officers before being issued a shapeless thin cotton dress, odd-size clogs or shoes, and a towel the size of a hankie.

During registration, all prisoners were given a colored cloth triangle according to their category plus the first letter of their country (*i.e.*, H for Holland) and a number. Sabine's triangle was red, for political prisoners, and her number was 24597. They would from now on be addressed only by their number.

From this point, the women were divided into those who were unfit to work and those who were useful as laborers. The old, the sick and the handicapped were instantly shot or gassed. In the autumn of 1944, a new gas chamber was built, and the camp changed from a labor camp to an extermination camp.

By the time Sabine arrived, the camp was already bursting at the seams. Most women had to share a bed, sleeping head to toe and sharing, if they were lucky, a blanket.

Being a *Nacht und Nebel* prisoner, and therefore considered extra-dangerous, she was sent to Barrack 32, a special *Nacht und Nebel* barrack, which already housed eight hundred women. During our visit, our guide took us to the area behind a fence where these barracks were situated. The outline of Barrack 32, at the far end of the camp, is still visible on the ground and is close to the big wall surrounding the whole camp.

During the war, these wooden buildings stood separate from other buildings behind a barbed wire fence and were extra-heavily guarded. Awful though it was, Sabine was lucky that she was not, like many other political prisoners, sent straight to the gas chamber.

For most of her time there, Sabine shared her narrow cot with Hetty de Stoppelaar, a student from Leiden, who had also worked for the Resistance. Friendships in the camp were vitally important for moral and actual support. Towards the end of the war, they would both be sent to Mauthausen and eventually come home to Holland together. Their mutual support during these grueling times resulted in a very strong lifelong friendship.

The first impression for the newcomers on arrival was the constant deafening noise. Loudspeakers blaring out marching songs and instructions, barking dogs, screaming guards, shouting, crying and the general noise of thousands of frightened women and children. The constant pushing and shoving as people tried to get out of the way of the guards and their dogs, escaping from a beating or running to roll call. The sense of panic and fear was constant and everywhere.

And then there was the stench. With the accumulation of thousands of unwashed people squashed together and the lack of sanitation, it was overpowering.

As all possessions had been taken away, it was vitally important to try and acquire some small items for daily survival. Every scrap of fabric or piece of string was of major importance. A spoon or a needle was a great luxury that had to be "bought" by exchanging your daily food ration. A small piece of fabric could be made into a small bag, worn under your dress to keep your spoon, comb or piece of soap in, either for your own use or as a bargaining tool for a bit of food that might make the difference between life or death. Everything had to be tied to your body or it would be stolen.

As Sabine later said in wonderment, "We were such a strange-looking group of women. Tufts of regrown hair, dirty, smelly, wearing shapeless dresses with odd-size shoes or boots, usually too big or too small."

Life from the time of arrival would consist of hard labor, standing for hours during roll calls in freezing temperatures, rain, wind and heat waves, half-starved and barely wearing any clothes.

★ ★ ★

All concentration camps followed the same rigid layout, based on a blueprint designed by Theodor Eicke, Commandant of Dachau, and built by Himmler. Barracks sat at right angles in rows along a straight, wide road that divided the camp in two. This *Lagerstraße* was made up of coal dust, cinders, gravel and mud and was often waterlogged. For the road leading to the camp, the ashes of murdered and burned prisoners were also used.

The barracks on either side of this thoroughfare were more than fifty meters long. A door in the middle of the long side divided them in two equal parts, an A-side and a B-side with, in between them, a small room for the *Blockälteste*, the person in charge, a wash area with twelve basins and twelve toilets, and a small living area with long tables. The dormitories initially housed around five hundred prisoners. When Sabine arrived, there were roughly eight hundred women, but as the war progressed, the numbers doubled and even trebled. They became so overcrowded that sitting while eating, or indeed sitting at any time, became a forgotten luxury. The beds, initially steel, later made of wood, were three bunks high and stood in units of three, making nine beds in a little group. Sleeping arrangements were head to toe to begin with, but this became impossible when up to five women had to share the narrow bed. Some were lucky and managed to obtain a thin straw mattress and perhaps a blanket to share. Others just had to sleep on the bare boards.

When my brother and I visited the camp, there was still one barrack standing, housing the remains of windows and walls of some other barracks. What struck me most of all was how thin the bits of wood from the walls were. Hardly thicker than plywood. It really brought home to me how much they must have suffered from the cold, which could be extreme in this climate.

Going to the latrines at night or during roll calls was forbidden. In fact, going to the toilet at any time required express permission. "If we got up in the night and touched the light switch, even by accident, we would be shot instantly," Sabine recalled. For those suffering from dysentery or feeling sick, this was torture, as it was for those sleeping below them.

On her second day in the camp, Sabine, along with many others, was marched to a large hall, where they were told their job: weaving clothes. The weaving mill was part of a large factory complex that made uniforms for the German army, supplying the Texled company, set up by the SS. There were even rabbit farms within the camp supplying the wool.

Sabine described the factory as a deafening inferno. Abuse was the order of the day. The three men in charge of the factory were sentenced to death after the war because of their terrible mistreatment of the prisoners.

Initially the work was in eight-hour shifts, but after an inspection by Himmler, this was increased to twelve hours per day, with half an hour rest. The machines were old-fashioned and very difficult to operate. The work required four separate actions in a specific sequence. "I couldn't do it," Sabine said. "I had a 40°C temperature and was feeling very sick." She was very worried she would be sent to the gas chamber due to lack of output, but after several days of struggling, she was instead sent to the *Revier* (hospital).

This was not as reassuring as it sounds. On the whole, the *Revier* was to be avoided at all costs. The chance of coming out alive was very small. On arrival, all patients were forced to stand naked in a freezing cold hall, doors wide open, waiting to be inspected by the doctor, who carefully kept his distance for fear of contagion. The inspection included teeth, which would be immediately extracted without anesthetics if not in good order. Any nits or lice led to instant loss of hair.

Sabine was sent to the typhoid room. Originally this room contained four beds, but when she arrived there, it held twenty-one beds, in tiers of three. Most beds had at least two patients in them. By now, apart from typhoid, she also suffered from bronchitis, angina pectoris, and serious ear and sinus infections. As a result, her eyes were permanently damaged. Before long, dysentery was added to her agony. All in all, she spent six weeks in the *Revier*.

After the war, she said, "Everyone but me thought I was going to die, and that made me feel determined to stay alive." Her memories of her stay in the *Revier* are hazy, but one memory stayed with her all her life. A young French girl, herself a patient, looked after her as she drifted in and out of consciousness and always sang "Mon Premier Rendez-vous." It was the title song of a film of the same name, which was a huge hit during the war in France. "I have always been so grateful to her, and after the war, during reunions, I tried to find her, but there is no record of her anywhere."

During the rest of that first winter in Ravensbrück, she also suffered from several bouts of flu. Her teeth too were giving her a lot of trouble, but while standing in line to see the dentist, she realized that his solution to any problem, like the doctor's, was to extract all teeth without anesthetics. She decided to suffer toothaches instead.

Sabine remembered the many dead, often three or four a day. Their naked bodies were dumped in the washing area. No medication was available to treat the patients.

Twice a week, the SS doctor would arrive. In Sabine's time, that was Dr. Treite, who would slowly walk down the line of patients waiting to be told who was to live and who was to die. The gynecologist Percival Treite became a member of the SS while still a student. After working at the Front for a while, he was moved to the women's camp because of his specialty. In 1947 he was sentenced to death because of his involvement with the sterilization experiments and his enthusiasm for selecting women for the gas chamber. He managed to commit suicide before the sentence was completed.

Every day, forced abortions and sterilizations were performed. Human experiments were tried out on prisoners by replicating conditions on the Front, in order to find a way of alleviating the wounds their own soldiers suffered while fighting. In order to achieve this, patients were injected with gas, gangrene, splinters of wood, glass, soil and pus, and then treated with sulfonamide drugs to see if their condition would improve. It never did.

Sabine shared her barrack with some eighty Polish women who were the main victims of these experiments. There were also experiments on regeneration of bones and removal of muscle tissue, resulting in lasting disabilities. Medical experiments were the order of the day, and if the patient did not die quickly enough, they were helped along with an injection. They all ended up crippled and had fainting fits, but how many died, Sabine didn't know nor say.

After six weeks in the *Revier*, Sabine was moved to a general sick block. The chance to be selected for the gas chamber was slightly less there. She soon picked up nits and lice as well. Every morning and evening she had to find time to get rid of at least some of them. A lost cause, as they bred faster than they could be removed. They added greatly to the pain, discomfort and infections suffered already, but she soon learned how to squeeze them between her nails and, like everyone else, inspected her fellow prisoners, rather like monkeys.

Somehow she had by now grown an inner core of steely determination that she almost certainly did not possess before the war. Her will to survive did not waver. The misery had weakened her physically, but mentally she was determined she was going to survive this. Perhaps her only bit of luck was that she did not have children, a sister or a mother with her.

She could concentrate on survival for herself only. And she was determined to live.

After her stay in the *Revier* and back in her own barrack, the days were long. In winter the prisoners had to get up at 3:20 a.m. and stand at attention in the big square from 3:30 until 7 a.m. They were not allowed to wear a blanket or extra clothing over their thin dresses. Some managed to get hold of some cardboard or paper to put under their dresses and in their shoes, but this was taking a great risk. Everyone had to stand in rows of ten (or two sets of five: for some reason the Germans liked their prisoners in groups of five), as female guards walked up and down the rows, counting everyone while screaming and threatening, accompanied by aggressively barking dogs.

It seemed endless, standing in the bitter cold, rain, wind and snow in the dark for hours and hours. On average it took four hours before the guards were satisfied that all prisoners were accounted for. If you had no job to go to or were being punished, you could be made to stand there for another few hours. It was therefore very important to be surrounded by your friends so that you could support each other at least mentally. If you fell down, you were taken away. Helping someone physically was strictly against the rules. Although forbidden to speak to each other, of course the women nevertheless did so whenever possible. I read that Sabine was a popular person to stand next to. She could talk endlessly about nothing much at all, although usually it was about food. The women all liked to talk about their favorite recipes. In this way she kept up the spirits of those around her and herself.

If there was time during the day, she would regularly run up to the barrack where her friend from The Hague, Lon Versteijnen, had been incarcerated for some time. Sabine would tap on the window, and the two of them would spend a little while gossiping, until Sabine was chased away. Lon said later: "She kept us going."

In a report for the Red Cross after the war, Sabine described how inadequate the food was in the camp, and as the war neared its end, it became even scarcer.

"When I arrived in November 1943 the ration at midday was a watery soup made from kohlrabi with added potato peelings and a slice of bread, often moldy. The evening meal was more or less the same and was also meant as breakfast. Often bits of earth, stones, straw, grass or insects were also found in the soup. As the war wore on, the evening soup was scrapped. On Sundays there would be no bread as it was not a workday. It was no wonder many women suffered from chronic diarrhea. The black watery coffee, awful as it tasted, was better than risking drinking from the camp's taps. The water was very contaminated."

Some prisoners were allowed to receive occasional parcels, but Sabine, as a *Nacht und Nebel* prisoner, and therefore to all intents and purposes dead, could not receive any. However, she was lucky that one of the other women, who was allowed a food parcel from home, was prepared to let Sabine choose some items for herself to add to her own next parcel. There was much hilarity when, apart from some food items she had asked for, a pair of pink bed socks and a pot of face cream were also included. It was clear that those at home had no idea of the conditions in the camp.

By autumn 1944, large groups of prisoners started to arrive from other camps, including, on September 9, a group of Dutch women. In the ten months Sabine had been there, the Dutch contingency had been small, but on that day, another 653 arrived. A hundred or so came from the jail in Scheveningen, near The Hague, but all the others came from Camp Vught, where they had been working at the Philips factory nearby and had been treated decently. They wore blue overalls with a red stripe and white scarves on their heads. They could not believe the scenes that greeted them in Ravensbrück. Nor could the women who were already imprisoned there believe their eyes seeing these well-dressed, well-fed women. I read a description of Sabine's reaction in another book:

> Sabine Zuur was completely enchanted when she saw them. She shouted a question to one of the women and immediately received some news from home, including the fact that her mother had started working for the Red Cross. Her two sons were in Japanese concentration camps in Indonesia and she had lost all contact with her daughter. She hoped to find out some news about all of them via the Red Cross.

How desperate Moeder Bien was for news of her daughter is obvious from her letter of December 23, 1943, written in very correct German and addressed to the commandant of the jail in Utrecht:

> I have been waiting in vain for a sign of life of my daughter since the 10th October.
>
> Perhaps you may remember the meeting we had recently on the 17th October, during which you gave me cause to believe that hopefully within a few weeks I might hear details about the whereabouts of my daughter.
>
> I hereby ask you to please help me to find out where to locate this information, which authority should I approach in the hope to get an answer as soon as possible?
>
> Hopefully you may understand how desperate I am not knowing the whereabouts of my only daughter. I also got news that my two sons are imprisoned in camps on Java.

I beg you again, as human being to human being, do
not leave my urgent request unanswered.

At Christmas, Moeder Bien received a reply, with the re-
mark that, from their end, the Kriegswehrmachtgefängnis
Utrecht could not give a satisfactory answer.

Short and to the point.

Moeder Bien had gone to work at a Red Cross depot where
parcels were made up for military prisoners of war. Her husband and middle son had died before the war, and her remaining
three children were all imprisoned in camps. Her colleagues at
the Red Cross managed to find out that Sabine was held in Ravensbrück. They made her their VIP prisoner. Every few weeks
they sent her a food parcel, none of which she ever received,
although the labels were sent back, marked Person Unknown.

The *Nacht und Nebel* system in practice.

The Hague suffered bombardments from time to time, and
in order to be prepared for the worst, Moeder Bien kept a small
suitcase with her most precious possessions by the front door.
When bombs were dropped nearby, she was in such a state of
panic that, hours later, she found herself wandering around
the streets, clutching the empty bottles that had been standing next to her case. When she eventually returned home,
the suitcase had survived and was still standing by the now-
demolished door and surrounded by the rubble of her house.

She was very lucky. The suitcase contained jewelry her husband had given her over the years. Now, with food so scarce,
she could use these pieces as a bargaining tool. She once told
me that she used to cycle, on wooden wheels, to the east of
Holland, where there were farms, and exchange diamond
earrings and a matching necklace for some butter, eggs and
milk. I was appalled, but she very reasonably explained that
you cannot eat diamonds. She survived the war, but with no
possessions to speak of.

The Siemens Factory

Many German manufacturers opened factories close to concentration camps, spotting an opportunity not only for cheap labor (they paid the German government a small sum for each worker), but also for an endless supply of workers who literally could be worked to death.

After her dismissal from hospital, Sabine worked for a few more weeks at the weaving machines, but then managed to get a job working in the Siemens factory, which was situated close to the camp. Siemens had built twenty barracks for this purpose. At that time, they were the biggest producers of electrical equipment for the armed forces. During our visit to Ravensbrück, our guide took us to the Siemens site where Sabine spent so many hours and which, as everywhere, is surrounded by trees and looks very peaceful now. There are no signs of the factory, apart from some outlines on the ground.

Work started at 7 a.m. and finished at 7 p.m., with a twenty-minute interval for "lunch." She had the nimble fingers required for this job—putting together parts for the V2-rockets.

As these would be used for the bombing of the homeland, there was much objection to doing this work. But actual objection or revolt was impossible. Guards with whips and dogs patrolled and inspected continuously for any sign of unrest or slacking. It was nevertheless a sought-after job, despite the lack of heating and the long hours. The main advantage was being able to sit down. The hard labor outside was much, much worse. Having a job also meant fewer hours standing around at the roll calls.

For the six months that Sabine worked in the factory, her job consisted of putting small types of batteries together for planes and submarines. Beatings and threats were the order of the day if work was going too slow.

At times, fellow workers suddenly disappeared and apparently were executed in the surrounding woods. The girl working next to Sabine disappeared just like that. One day she was gone.

But Sabine's stroke of good fortune came to an end when she was moved to the Instandsetzung 1, loading and unloading trains that came from the east, Russia and Poland. These at first carried uniforms from the Front that had to be cleaned and repaired before being sent back.

Sabine worked with three other Dutch women in her shift. Apart from the uniforms, there were many heavy leather overcoats lined with sheepskin. "They were very heavy, and we had to carry three in each hand, take them to a big hall and stack them. One day we had to move some heavy wooden crates, but they wouldn't shift. We were too tired and too weak, although we tried and tried. The *Unterscharführer* was standing next to me, impatiently flicking his rubber stick against his boot. Suddenly he grabbed me by my neck and shook me. When he let go, I fell to the ground, and he kicked me with his boot. I tried not to cry and with a straight face got up, only for him to repeat this another three or four times. When he finally walked away, my two fellow prisoners were frozen with shock and fear. I ran to our latrine and sat there crying for some time, not from the pain but from shock."

Sabine worked in the Instandsetzung 1 for nine months.

As the Russians started to invade Poland and forced the Germans to retreat, they looted every house, business, museum, hospital and castle they passed on their way back and filled the trains going west towards Berlin with paintings, gold, silver, jewelry, furs, carpets, in fact anything they could lay their hands on. The trains stopped at Ravensbrück, which lay on the main line to Berlin, for cataloging everything before going on to Berlin.

To one of her friends, Sabine said, "They are emptying Poland."

In the beginning, there would be a couple of trains per week, but as the war dragged on and the Germans were forced to retreat further, more and more trains started to arrive, up to twenty-six a day, with many cars each.

When it was discovered that she had been a secretary, Sabine was ordered to also type lists of all the goods on incoming trains. Her twelve-hour shift became a much longer shift.

Her little office, which she shared with three other women, was next to that of *Oberscharführer* Geisler and *Unterscharführers* Spier and Mozek. They supervised the women very strictly. Geisler sat opposite her, his desk pushed against hers. He shouted a lot, but Sabine was not intimidated. Later she said, "Barking dogs don't bite."

Her job consisted of noting down the number of the train and the car and then itemizing the entire contents and transferring each item on a list in her office. As the number of trains increased, it became impossible to keep up, and she resorted to first leaving out some cars from her lists, but later on she started leaving out whole trains. She was well aware that this was very risky, but it was physically not possible to deal with the volume of trains and goods. Inaccuracy was severely punished. "Punishment in the bunker was always a threat, and was much worse than just being shot dead."

The Germans were sticklers for accurate administration. Luckily her boss was also worn-out trying to keep up with the quantities arriving, so he was no longer checking her very carefully.

One of the other women in her office was Wanda, an older Polish countess from Krakow. Her eighteen-year-old daughter was also in the camp, having to carry the heavy soup containers to and from the barracks. Wanda's desk was next to Sabine's, and she also had to type lists. As she had never worked in her life, she was only able to type slowly with one finger. She had been very lucky to be sent out to work, as most older women were sent straight to the gas chamber. Despite Sabine barely being able to keep up her own workload, she helped Wanda as much as she could. They both knew what would befall Wanda if it was discovered she did not pull her weight. I do not know how long, with Sabine's help, she managed to hold on to this job, or if she even survived.

Meanwhile the working hours became longer and longer. What had started as a twelve-hour working day eventually became a twenty-two- to twenty-three-hour working day; sometimes there was barely time to sleep even two hours, but Sabine stayed positive and efficient in her support for others.

One day, while sorting through the stolen goods, she came across a beautiful gold powder compact. In the grimness of the camp, it must have been a magical thing of beauty. She told me that, to her dying day, she did not know what came over her, but she took it and hid it under her clothes and then in the back of a drawer in her desk. Not many days after, she entered her office to find a young German soldier holding the compact. He had been checking her desk. Sabine knew that theft was punishable by death, so her terror was immense. But just then, some other soldiers came into the room, and he quickly put the compact in his pocket. Even theft by Germans warranted a severe punishment, so Sabine was very relieved. He could not betray her, and she could not betray him, but they both remained wary of each other.

In between all the misery of daily life, there were small moments of satisfaction. "We got a short period of rest in the middle of the day to eat our ration of soup and bread, which we spent sitting behind one of the wagons while eating off beautiful china plates taken from the trains and which we smashed afterwards to prevent them going to Berlin. The soup was eaten with monogrammed silver spoons, which we buried in the mud. Our small effort at sabotage."

Developments
at the Front

During the winter of 1944, the Russian army made great advances. The Front was pushed back further west towards northern Germany, and Ravensbrück was in their sight line. In June, the invasion in Normandy had landed, and the net tightened around the Germany army and Berlin.

The concentration camps on the routes of the Red Army started emptying and sending their prisoners to camps not yet liberated. In Ravensbrück, they arrived in their thousands from the camps in the east. Ravensbrück was already full to bursting and had no room to house them. The new arrivals were therefore kept outside the walls, without shelter, food, bedding or any sort of sanitation. The camp inmates were thrown into even further despair seeing the deprivations of the newcomers, which were even worse than their own. Many had traveled for days on end, in midwinter, in open coal cars, barely clothed and without any food or water. Only after a few days, some tents were erected and a few receptacles were put around for toilets.

The resident Dutch prisoner group took immediate action to try and get at least some clothing for these poor souls, and Sabine, together with her friend Truus, stole quantities of clothes from the warehouse depots to hand to the new arrivals. There was already a great sense that the war could not last much longer. The Germans obviously felt the same. Discipline began to relax.

The sense of losing the war affected the Germans strongly, and they started to think of their own future and the importance of being able to show the liberators how well they had looked after their prisoners. Suddenly buildings were improved and "hospitals" built, and the women were allowed to wear extra clothing. Headscarves were no longer obligatory.

Sabine, to her delight, even found her old honey-colored cord trousers back in the clothing storage. Although food and conditions generally deteriorated, hope had revived, and the urgency to survive until the end of the war was everywhere.

As the Red Army got nearer, the authorities in Ravensbrück began to panic and decided to try and empty the camp and leave as little evidence as possible. Since they could not kill enough people fast enough, a second gas chamber was built in Ravensbrück, opening in March 1945. Both crematorium and gas chambers were working day and night in the last three months of the war. At least 5,000 women and children were gassed in those last few weeks, but even two gas chambers and a crematorium were not enough to deal with the numbers being sent to their death. Many were killed and burnt in the nearby woods.

This terrible month was Sabine's last one in Ravensbrück. The killing was not going fast enough, and the decision was made to start sending prisoners to other camps further south, some on death marches, during which thousands died, and some by cattle trains, including 2,000 women and children to

Mauthausen, of whom only thirty-seven, including Sabine, were Dutch.

On March 1, 1945, the order came for all *Nacht und Nebel* prisoners to go immediately to the punishment block, where they were joined by Roma and Jewish women and children. Two thousand of them were jammed into the cell blocks, all windows and doors were closed and locked, and they were left in total darkness, surrounded by heavy security. No water, food or sanitation was provided. No room to lie or sit down, which led to bloody fights and endless piercing screaming. Mass hysteria took hold, as the women knew that the punishment block was always the prelude to the gas chambers. The fact that there were Jewish and Roma women among them made it a certainty.

But it was not the end. The following morning, after a horrendous night, the women were marched to the trains and taken south.

Sabine spent from November 1, 1943, until March 2, 1945, in Ravensbrück. Now another hell awaited her.

Ravensbrück to Mauthausen

As the crow flies, Mauthausen is some 700 km from Ravensbrück, but by train traveling through a bombed Germany and Austria, the journey was nearer 1,000 km and took three or four days, since the train stopped frequently.

Sabine described her journey to Mauthausen in a variety of reports and excerpts for the Red Cross and to author Dunya Breuer:

"The following morning, we were marched to the train station and pushed into cattle and coal wagons, around seventy women per wagon. The only way was to stand up or lie across each other, legs pulled up as much as possible, causing terrible cramps and stiffness. The *Aufseherin*, the woman in charge, and the guard sat by a small oil lamp and demanded a space around them, as they were worried they might catch our lice and nits, thus making the place even more cramped. A small metal bucket was provided by way of a toilet. It frequently had to be emptied through a small gap in the doors by some unfortunate sitting near there.

"On departure we were given one large piece of bread and a surrogate sausage, but since we did not know how long our journey would be, it was difficult to decide how much to eat and how much to save and for how long. Of course, if you saved it, the chance of it being stolen while you were asleep was great.

"The wagons were not only filthy with coal dust, but also freezing cold. Despite traveling in a southerly direction, the weather did not get any warmer. Occasionally the train stopped, and we were allowed to get off to relieve ourselves underneath the train.

"In our wagon, there was a woman who had gone mad and who constantly tried to run away. After having caught and beaten her several times, the guards tied her by her wrists to the open sliding doors, her feet barely touching the ground. It was very distressing seeing her hanging there like Jesus on the Cross.

"We managed to remove a plank from the side of our wagon so that we could see the passing landscape. We traveled through Berlin, which in March 1945 looked very sinister, like a ghost town with blackened, bombed buildings covered in dirty snow. The few people we saw did not look in much better condition than we were ourselves. It was an eerie sight.

"After four days, we finally arrived in the middle of the night at a small, quiet station, exhausted and starving. The dead were removed, and those women too weak to stand were taken to the back of the train and shot. I remember the shots.

"In moonlight and through heavy snow, we were forced to start our march in groups of five, carrying whatever possessions we had. A lorry drove behind us, picking up the bodies of those who succumbed on the way. We walked through several villages and hamlets, but nothing moved anywhere. I looked up at the bedroom windows and, seeing no one, I wondered if people were too scared to look, or were they too used to seeing these pitiful processions and slept through them?

"One of my worst memories is that of a Roma or Jewish woman carrying one child and holding the hand of another, who walked a few rows ahead of me. She was exhausted and kept falling down. The SS guards threatened and beat her, and the others around her tried to help her up, until the guards got fed up and dragged her to the end of the line and shot her. The other women took her hysterical children with them.

"We were all so afraid to fall down and not be able to get up again. We knew what would happen."

Terror and an iron willpower to survive kept these women going. I have often wondered how some managed to survive these horrors, while others gave up or went mad.

Perhaps it was by thinking only of the next step, the next hour or day, and perhaps complete detachment, and with calm fatalism accepting the awful reality of what was going on around them. Thinking or feeling made you weak.

Sabine said later, "After the war, I buried these memories, but later they came back. It seems only then you begin to realize all the things that happened to you."

Mauthausen

Konzentrationslager Mauthausen

Adolf Hitler spent a large part of his youth in the small provincial town of Linz in Austria. He had big plans to turn it into a glorious *Führerstadt*.

From Linz, a bus ride of about forty-five minutes along the Donau River brings you to the spot where Hitler envisaged his grandiose building plans as his legacy for his thousand-year Reich: Konzentrationslager Mauthausen.

Three months after my visit to Ravensbrück, I am on my way to visit Mauthausen. It is a sunny autumn day, and the area, like that around Ravensbrück, is also beautiful.

With me I have a large envelope with all the letters written by Franz Josef Gebele, a German prisoner, and addressed to my mother.

Apart from wanting to see the camp for myself, I also hope to find out more about this mystery man.

The building of a labor camp in Mauthausen was started in March 1938, close to a granite quarry. Over the next few years, another hundred or so smaller camps were built in the vicinity of the main camp. Of those, the three Gusen camps were the most notorious ones.

In the beginning, Mauthausen housed mainly political prisoners or criminals who had previously been imprisoned in Dachau. As the war dragged on, Mauthausen, originally a labor camp, became an extermination camp for Resistance fighters and political activists from all over Europe.

Hitler's dreams for his thousand-year Reich started here at the granite quarry in Mauthausen. The granite was mined under the most unimaginable circumstances, and in the seven years of its existence, more than 320,000 people were used as slave laborers, of whom only around 80,000 survived the war.

Although the outside world did not know what was happening in the concentration camps at the time, the name Mauthausen even then already evoked great fear. Nothing was ever heard again of people sent there. It is described as one of the deadliest of all concentration camps.

Camp Mauthausen was established on the top of a high hill on the outskirts of the town. The infamous quarry at the foot of the mountain was called the "Wiener Graben" after the upmarket shopping street in the old center of Vienna. It was an ironic nickname. The contrast between the two places could not have been greater. Thousands met their death in the Mauthausen Wiener Graben. My mother often spoke about the infamous *Todesstiege* (death stairs) that connect the quarry with the camp above.

In the war, the 186 uneven treads of this staircase, hewn out of rocks, were barely manageable, particularly after rain or with icy conditions. Prisoners were forced to climb the thirty-meter-high staircase carrying blocks of granite of up to 50 kg on their backs, SS guards chasing them up from behind. Any stumble or fall would result in a kick over the side. Often the men were tied together, so that if one fell, he would

take the other one with him. It would create a domino effect all the way down to the bottom. If they did make it to
the top, they were often executed anyway or pushed over the
edge to the great excitement of the watching officers on the
other side of the quarry. They called these involuntary jump-
ers "parachutists."

This practice obviously upset some neighboring farmers, as
one of them wrote a letter to the county commissioner in Perg
complaining about the inhumane treatment of the prisoners:

> In the concentration camp Mauthausen at the work site
> in Vienna ditch, inmates are being shot repeatedly; those
> badly struck live yet for some time, and so remain lying
> next to the dead for hours, even half a day long.
>
> My property lies upon an elevation next to the Vienna
> ditch, and one is often an unwilling witness to such out-
> rages. I am sickly and such a sight makes such a demand
> on my nerves that in the long run I cannot bear this.
>
> I request that it be arranged that such inhumane deeds
> be discontinued, or else be done where one does not
> see it.

Now that I see the staircase with my own eyes, a feeling
of sheer horror overwhelms me, even though the staircase
has been improved and renewed and all treads are now even
and safe. Unlike many other visitors, I cannot bring myself to
climb it. My mother was an involuntary witness to the many
horrors that took place there on a daily basis.

Today Mauthausen is still a small provincial town and is
probably only known worldwide for its connection to the
cruel history of the camp.

From the station it is a few kilometers' walk to the foot of
the mountain, where the road begins to climb steeply. I arrive

by car, but I wonder how the exhausted women and children managed this walk in the middle of the winter, at night after days of traveling with very little food, thin clothing and ill-fitting shoes, if any at all. They must all have had iron will-power to accomplish this feat.

Nowadays the camp is clean and quiet, but still, a feeling of oppression comes over me as I enter through the gate. I am taken aback by the sheer size of the camp. It takes several hours to walk around it.

A few of the buildings are still there: some of the original barracks, the *Kommandantur* (command headquarters), the laundry, the kitchen, the *Revier*, the crematorium and the gas chamber.

Walking around this large and empty-looking area, I have trouble trying to imagine the chaos, the cruelty and the ever-increasing masses of desperate people swirling around in the last weeks and days of the war.

Inside the wall surrounding the camp, as well as in a large area outside, there are memorials, representing the countries from which the victims originated. A mixture of desperation, fear and dejection overwhelms me when I read the inscription on the big marble statue within the camp of the Russian general Dmitri Karbyshev. He died on the night of February 17 to 18, 1945, aged sixty-four, after having stood naked for hours during roll call, accompanied by several hundred of his Soviet soldiers and having been sprayed with cold water until he and his soldiers slowly froze to death. Karbyshev would not give in and kept encouraging his fellow victims, while looking his enemy straight in the eyes. He stayed up-right until the end.

When I walk through the gate, I try to imagine what my mother must have felt when she first entered Mauthausen. She herself remembered it clearly:

"Mauthausen is situated on a high hill. After having walked for several hours, we finally arrived. Our first sight was of the big entrance gate, topped by a *Hakenkreuz* and a large eagle, lit up by searchlights. The oppressive fear I felt then will always stay with me. We were herded onto a large square and had to stand there till morning. Eventually a fierce-looking group of SS guards took us to the underground laundry. We knew what to expect: this was the moment we would be gassed."

Sabine watched the first group of women being taken downstairs, but when they reappeared after a while, there was a feeling of great relief, causing some nervous laughing. The emerging women had been relieved of their own clothes and were all wearing oversized men's clothes. But one of the women shouted, "Just you wait. When you have been downstairs, you won't be laughing anymore."

Once downstairs they had to get undressed and, naked, stand on a step while male prisoners walked around with a bucket and large brush and painted the women with disinfectant between their legs and under their arms. After that, they had to put their heads in a bucket of disinfectant, "but so many nits and lice floated around in it that you picked up more than you left behind," Sabine recounted. She managed to escape this ordeal by claiming she had already been "done."

The showers were next, and fear returned, but luckily only a trickle of water came out. All the time the women had to run the gauntlet of the sneering officers, who were pointing and making rude remarks. The men's clothes they were given were of course far too big. Sabine was given a pair of shorts that sagged down to her knees, but when she asked for a safety pin, there was only mocking laughter.

A general health check followed. Of course, all women assured the interrogators that they were in excellent health and ready to do any type of work. Sabine, like all the others, was

exhausted and starved after sixteen months in Ravensbrück
and the terrible journey to Mauthausen. On top of that, she
now also had pneumonia and jaundice. But she also insisted
she was in good health. The gas chamber was right next door.

The march through the male barracks to the three female-
designated quarantine barracks was a trial. As Mauthausen
had been a male camp only, the prisoners had hardly seen
any women for years, and this column of 2,000 or so strange-
looking women and children marching through was a major
event. According to one report, the barracks were sagging to
one side with the number of men hanging out of the doors
and windows to watch this parade.

Amstetten

Sabine said, "In our barrack the beds were arranged in units of nine, three by three with four people per bed. All night long people fell or were pushed out of bed. There was a lot of screaming and shouting. The windows were not allowed to be opened due to fear of spreading illness. We could not move due to overcrowding, and we waited and waited." This was probably up to two weeks. Sabine could not remember, but around March 20, they were suddenly moved to a barrack just outside the camp, near the Wiener Graben, and divided into groups. Here there were no beds, just straw on the floor to sleep on. Finally they were told what their job would be: clearing bombed railway lines and junctions at Amstetten, near Linz. To get there, they had to get up at 2 a.m. and march for two hours. Amstetten had suffered a bombing raid of more than two hundred bombs by the Americans a few days before, and the women were sent to clear the resulting chaos.

It was very dangerous work, as every day brought new bombardments. Of course there were plenty of replacement prisoners waiting to take over from those who died.

Sabine said, "We were given enormous shovels and pitch-forks, which we could barely lift, let alone the heavy rails and sleepers, which were the beams the tracks were laid upon.

"But on our first day, before too long, the air raid siren sounded, and panicked guards drove us over the fields up a wooded hill. The sun was shining and spring was in the air, and while the bombardment was all around us, we felt elated. We were outside the camp and in the fresh air. A small sense of freedom came over us as we watched the railway carriages flying through the air.

"'At least we don't have to clear those away anymore,' the women noted. Eventually, though, the planes were flying lower and coming straight at us, and the bombs started dropping all around us. I cannot describe what it feels like to see them coming straight at you. One of the nearby trees fell on top of me, but so much stuff was raining down, I did not even notice it. Eighty women were killed on that first day. They were hanging in bits off trees, buried under earth and trees. Many had gone mad with fear. We did not know what to do. The guards who, in first instance, had run away, returned when the bombing had stopped and made us collect the dead. The women dug out a young girl, barely alive, who had gone mad."

A nearby farmer brought some schnapps for the women while they were counted. After some time, the dead and seri-ously wounded, including Sabine, were put on an open horse-drawn wagon filled with straw and taken back via Linz to Mauthausen. They got stuck in a large square in Linz, where a furious shouting and threatening crowd had gathered. Sa-bine managed to pull herself up, tapped a nearby man on the shoulder, and asked him, *"Was ist los hier?"* The pilot and crew of a shot-down bomber, who had jumped to safety by parachute, had been captured and were being paraded in the square. The locals wanted revenge for the bombardment. "It was a terrible sight," said Sabine. "He was probably lynched, but he only did his duty, after all."

It took hours to get back to Mauthausen, and quite a few more died on the way. Back in the camp, a quarantine barrack was used as a hospital for some of the wounded, although there was no nursing and no medication. One of Sabine's friends, Riek de Geus, was badly wounded and lived for another three days in intense distress, crying for her mother until she died. She was twenty-four years old.

A small camp hospital was built in Mauthausen towards the end of the war in order to give the impression, when the Allies came into the camp, that the sick had been cared for. Sabine was one of the lucky ones to be taken to this hospital by Russian stretcher-bearers.

Despite the terrible circumstances in this hastily improvised hospital, her broken ankle was expertly set by Professor Pot-laker from Prague, himself a prisoner for thirteen years already.

Gebele

While the wounded were lying in the corridors, waiting for treatment, a few of the male prisoners approached them and handed out food that they themselves had received in parcels from home.

One male prisoner who approached Sabine was Franz Josef Gebele. He was in the hospital himself while recovering from a bullet wound as well as being an orderly there. He offered to help her in any way he could. He seems to have instantly taken a great liking to Sabine, and she, finding someone who for the first time in years was kind and wanted to help her and look after her and, more to the point, was able to do so, gratefully received his attentions and food offerings. She probably felt she could accept his help because, although he was a hated German, he himself was also a prisoner and in the camp against his will. Sabine was still in a state of shock from the bombing, the ensuing panic and her injuries.

Gebele told her that he came from München (Munich) and had already been a prisoner for eleven years, and in that time he had gained the trust of the guards. Mauthausen was only opened in 1938, so where he was imprisoned before, I have not been able to find out. Perhaps Dachau, as that was a criminal jail before the war. In documents he is variously described as Franz Gebele or Franz Joseph (or Josef) or even Johann Joseph, which makes it difficult to trace him. I was however, able to establish the reason he was there, but Sabine at this time of course did not know. He was a *Berufsverbrecher*, a career criminal. He wore a green triangle, indicating he was a thief.

After Sabine had been treated for her wounds and left the hospital to return to her own barrack, Gebele smuggled letters to her via the Russian stretcher-bearers (also prisoners themselves) and she, in return, smuggled letters back to him on paper he supplied.

I found a bundle of seventeen of his letters, some typed, but most handwritten in the last few weeks of the war. In a note with them, she had written, "These letters are written by Franz Josef Gebele, a German prisoner of war who had already been imprisoned for eleven years and who fell in love with me and saved my life."

Sabine's letters are lost, but Gebele's letters offer a fascinating glimpse of life in a concentration camp in the last few weeks of the war as well as being a strange kind of love letters. After eleven years living in the most dire circumstances, he was a desperate and damaged man.

It took me some time and effort to find someone who could translate these letters for me since they are written in the old-fashioned *Sütterlin* script no longer used, and while the handwriting itself is beautiful, it is very difficult to read.

Initially, on reading the letters, I felt a great dislike for Gebele, and the fear my mother must have felt was tangible. With every letter, he fell more and more obsessively in love with her, and yet at the same time, there was always a slight threat,

Top: Bientje (Sabine), aged 3 in 1921. *Bottom:* Sabine, aged 4, with her brothers Loek, Joop and Han in 1922.
Photo Credits: Author's personal archive.

Sabine, aged 14.
Photo Credit: Author's personal archive.

Moeder Bien and Sabine in The Hague.
Photo Credit: Author's personal archive.

Sabine (in the middle) with friends on the beach, July 1940.
Photo Credit: Author's personal archive.

With friends on the beach in Scheveningen. Erik Hazelhoff Roelfzema in middle in the back. August 1939.
Photo Credit: Author's personal archive.

Sabine sailing on the lakes near The Hague, beginning of the war.
Photo Credit: Author's personal archive.

Photo of Sabine taken by Gerard Vinkesteijn a few months before they were arrested. Photo Credit: Author's personal archive.

Sabine in 1940.
Photo Credit: Author's personal archive.

Taro Roeper Bosch, taken in Zeeland, 1940, around the time of the mobilization. Photo Credit: Author's personal archive.

Gerard Vinkesteijn, Wassenaar—betrayed and arrested.
Photo Credit: Author's personal archive.

Eighty-three love letters written by Taro to Sabine in 1940.
Photo Credit: Author's personal archive.

Sabine and Gerard in his garden in Wassenaar. Photo taken by Broer Moonen. June 22, 1941.
They were in the same resistance group. **Photo Credit: Author's personal archive.**

Ik hoop dat U het
goed maakt, lieverd?
Tot ziens hoor,
Omhelsd en héél veel
kussen van
        Sabine

Groeten aan alle
huisgenooten e.a.

$\frac{5}{2}$

AFZ. S. Zuur. Cel 2/1
Havenstraat 6 – A'dam.

Mevrouw S.H. Zuur-
        Schlette.
Van Alkemadelaan 49
    's-Gravenhage.

A'dam, 16 Aug. 1943

Liefste Mams!
        Momenteel ben ik "reinigster"
en omdat ik als zoodanig veel loopen
moet, zou ik graag willen dat U a.s.
Vrijdag, gelijk met het pakketje (dat
ik nu ook weer elke week hebben mag
    en de wasch m'n donkerbl. schoenen m
de crêpe-zolen stuurt en als 't kan een
paar sandalen met houten zolen (maat
38½ of 39) voor me koopt. Dit is voor 't
dweilen. M'n bruine schoenen stuur
ik dan terug om te verzolen (de schoen
maker van Bep R.)
        Stuurt U m'n onlpen ook in de wasch?

Two official letters from Sabine to Moeder Bien, written in Amsterdam jail. August 16, 1943.
Photo Credit: Author's personal archive.

Ontvangstbewijs voor een Persoonsbewijs

Heden ingenomen een Persoonsbewijs, genummerd _____/_____

uitgereikt te _____ aan

_____, geboren

op _____ te _____ thans

opgenomen in het bevolkingsregister van _____

Gedaan te _____ op _____ 194_

De ambtenaar,
(onderteekening en functie)

11024

K 599

SICHERHEITSPOLIZEI - SD - EINSATZKOMMANDO
Dienststelle der Feldpostnummer:

S D

Alle polizeilichen Behörden werden ersucht Inhaber dieses Ausweises

Herrn.

von der Dienstelle der Feldposteinheit   nötigenfalls Schutz

und Hilfe zu gewähren.

Ausgefertigt am _____ 194

(Unterschrift, Dienstgrad, Dienststellung)

Peter Kaiser, Paris. 8, Rue Taitbout.

STAATSBEDRIJF DER POSTERIJEN, TELEGRAFIE EN TELEFONIE 3

IDENTITEITSBEWIJS VOOR

NAAM EN VOORNA(A)M(EN)
GEBOREN _____ TE _____
RANG
STANDPLAATS
AMBULANT
AANWIJZING OMTRENT UNIFORM
WOONPLAATS EN HUISADRES
AFGEGEVEN DEN _____ 194_

HANDTEEKENING VAN DEN HOUDER:

HET HOOFD VAN DIENST
INSPECTEUR, DISTRICTHOOFD, DIRECTEUR.

HANDTEEKENING:

STAATSBEDRIJF DER POSTERIJEN, TELEGRAFIE EN TELEFONIE

IDENTITEITSBEWIJS VOOR

NAAM EN VOORNA(A)M(EN)
GEBOREN _____ TE _____
RANG
STANDPLAATS
AMBULANT
AANWIJZING OMTRENT UNIFORM
WOONPLAATS EN HUISADRES
AFGEGEVEN DEN _____ 194_

HANDTEEKENING VAN DEN HOUDER:

HET HOOFD VAN DIENST
INSPECTEUR, DISTRICTHOOFD, DIRECTEUR.

HANDTEEKENING:

Uitgereikt te 's-Gravenhage

den 31.December 1943

Che.. den Alg.Staf.

Dit legitimatiebewijs is slechts geldig, indien voorzien van een zegel in de kleur en met den opdruk van het betreffende kwartaal

LEGITIMATIEBEWIJS

Naam: van Dam

Voornamen: Theodorus

Geboortedatum: 19.Mei 1905

Rang: Inspecteur der Rijksrecherche

Dienstnummer: H.C. 18

Volgnummer: 583

VERLENGING RIJKSDIENSTKAART
NEDERLANDSCHE SPOORWEGEN

Verlengingskaart D **5043**

Hr.
Mw.

K 2347

2e KLASSE

Forged documents, possibly used by Sabine's resistance group. From her archive.
Photo Credit: Author's personal archive.

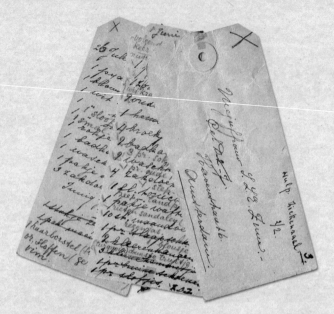

Three laundry lists. Two of them have an X, marking a secret letter is enclosed in the laundry.
In pencil on the middle label, it says "lots of kisses, S" in letters to MBien.

Gericht
des Kommandierenden General..
und Befehlshabers der Truppen
des Heeres in den Niederlanden
   St.L. I Nr. 107/43

O.U., den 22. Oktober 1943.

An Frau

   S.H. Zuur - Schlette

      D e n   H a a g
      ----
      van Alkemadelaan 49

   Auf Ihre Anfrage vom 19. 10. 1943 wird mitgeteilt,
dass nach den bestehenden Bestimmungen in der angegebenen
Strafsache keine Auskunft erteilt werden kann.

                              Oberkriegsgerichtsrat.

Reply by the Oberkriegsgerichtsrat to Moeder Bien regarding her request for information
about her daughter. October 22, 1943.

voor mij op. Neem zooveel als ze willen geven, de bonnen of 't geld geef ik U later terug. Als ik thuiskom eet ik dan alle koekjes achter mekaar op. Ik verheug me er nu maar vast op. 't water komt al in m'n mond als ik aan een oudetje met kaas of een custard-bla'tje denk, laat staan een rijsttafel in Tampat Senang!

Wilt U me nog sturen: m'n rieten schoenen (op kantoor) Sunlight zeep (1 stuk maar, vraag 't aan Cees, die kan 't krijgen van Ernst O.) m'n regenjas, en verder wat ik op de label erbij schreef. En maar 1x in de maand verband en een andere step-in en een

U kunt ze overal in stoppen, ik pluis toch alles uit elkaar. Bij de contrôle doen ze dat ook wel, maar daar moeten ze ruim 200 wasschen nakijken alleen al voor onze (Duitsche) vrouwen-afdeeling; dus allicht heb ik een kans. Doe er ook s.v.p. iets goedkoops maar eetbaars in en verstop dat ook in een maandverband of 200. Vooral niets duurs of zeldzaams want de kans dat het doorkomt is 1 op 5. U kunt b.v. stroop of kunsthoning in een leege Viva mel-flesch doen of boter in een leege tube tandpasta & dit is Leo goed toevertrouwd; zulke werkjes kan hij prima. Nu tro geen map ik hebben, vraag dit maar aan Carolientje, dat wil ik hier dol-graag hebben! Zorg dat het papier van Uw briefjes niet meer kraakt, Rol het op en wrijf het dan goed. Misschien kunnen Ton of Leo of Guus Oster ook wel eens mijn wasch hier halen of brengen of Bep R. misschien, dan hoeft U niet steeds, Mammie, want U zult 't wel

Letters from the Amsterdam jail written on cigarette paper and smuggled out in the laundry to Moeder Bien. May 30, 1943.

Gefangenbuch Nr. *1101*

Name: *Zeur*

Vorname: *Sabine Louise*

Geburtsdatum: *15. 7. 1918*

Religion: *engl.*

Tag der Einlieferung: *25. Aug. 43*

Aktenzeichen: *St. L. I 107/43*

Zuständiges Gericht: *Heer*

Straftat: *Spionage u. Feindbegünstig.*

Strafdauer:

Strafbeginn:

Strafende:

Sabine's identity card, which hung in her cell in Utrecht jail.
Photo Credit: Author's personal archive.

Weaving factory in Ravensbrück, taken in the beginning of the war.
Photo Credit: Horst Severens. Used with permission.

Slave laborers working in Ravensbrück.
Photo Credit: © Mahn- und Gedenkstätte Ravensbrück. Used with permission.

Camp Ravensbrück, circa 1940.
Photo Credit: Horst Severens. Used with permission.

Short note from Gebele to Sabine in Mauthausen.
Photo Credit: Author's personal archive.

Bottom: Letter from Gebele to "Sabine Sonnenschein" in Mauthausen.
Photo Credit: Author's personal archive.

Left: Wedding photo of Sabine and Peter Tazelaar, December 12, 1946, in Amsterdam.

Right: Moeder Bien, October 1949.

Photo Credits: Author's personal archive.

Left: From left to right: Sabine, unknown man, Hetty de Stoppelaar and Lon Versteijnen, just after the war.

Right: Sabine, Eva and Peter on the beach in Karachi, 1948.

Photo Credits: Author's personal archive.

Sabine, Peter Jr. and Eva in Scheveningen, 1953.

Photo Credit: Author's personal archive.

Peter, Eva and Sabine, 1948.

Photo Credit: Author's personal archive.

Peter Jr., Sabine and Eva, 1954.

Photo Credit: Author's personal archive.

Tazelaar family, Christmas 1951.

Photo Credit: Author's personal archive.

The Hague, 1955.
Photo Credit: Author's personal archive.

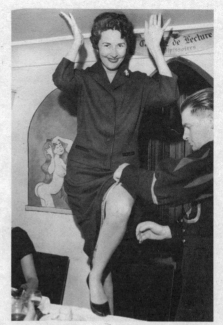

Sabine in a playful mood, end of the 1950s.
Photo Credit: Author's personal archive.

Zuur family in Scheveningen, January 1, 1929. Left to right: Loek, Father Louis, Sabine, Moeder Bien, Joop and Han.
Photo Credit: Author's personal archive.

Left: Gerard Dogger and Peter Tazelaar on their way back to England via the overland escape route, Winter 1942.
Photo Credit: Author's personal archive.

Bottom: Peter and Eric accompanying the queen back to Holland after the war.
Photo Credit: BNA Photographic / Alamy Stock Photo.

meant as a joke, but in the context of the camp surroundings, nevertheless a threat, in most of his letters.

But the more I read them, the more I felt pity and gratefulness for him. He did save her life, after all, by preventing her being sent to the gas chamber, which, after having broken her ankle and being unable to work, was a real possibility. He provided her with food, medication, and clothes, and protected her from the advances (or worse) of the guards and other prisoners.

The war was nearing its end, and the tension in the camp was very high. Discipline slackened, and more and more fights broke out between the prisoners, all desperate to survive, being so close to liberation. After years of extreme hardship and dehumanization, many had turned into savage animals.

Although Gebele constantly assured Sabine of his love, his letters are written formally, even after Sabine suggested right in the beginning that they should abandon the formal *Sie* and use the more personal *du* instead.

His first letter to her is undated, but was written shortly after the bombardment and after she had left the *Revier*.

Sehr Geehrtes Fräulein Zuur,
On the basis of our conversation earlier today I permit myself the freedom to importune you with a few lines and should not wish to miss the opportunity to ask you, honored lady, for the address of your dear mother for a purpose which I imagine you will clearly recall (from our conversation).

Please let me have the full address including that of her emergency accommodation, and I promise that you need have no concern whatsoever about what I shall arrange for your benefit. In addition I wanted to ask you most earnestly for your date and place of birth as well as your profession, I should be grateful if you please would not attempt to draw me on the purpose behind the request for the moment, but perhaps to return to it later when you are restored to freedom. I must be open and honest and admit that a sincere interest in your person has strongly attracted me to you after my being permitted to get to know you a little personally. Please do not interpret my forwardness in writing to you as effrontery and I particularly do not wish to exploit your status as a detainee or turn your head in any way. I believe I recall having told you who and what I am. If you will, grant me assent to permit me to be allowed to express myself in greater detail and greater depth, but, above all, you must first become well once more and to that end I would like to ask you from the bottom of my heart to grant me permission to contribute to your recuperation insofar as it is within my limited powers and given my insignificance in the camp. To that end I should put myself entirely at your disposal and ask accordingly that you should make full use of me. I ask you once more that you please excuse this letter and, if I may be so bold, ask [you] to treat it with discretion. In the meantime it is a matter of some urgency that I should like to speak with you in private and in person.

With heartfelt greetings and best wishes for a swift recovery,

Yours Franz Josef Gebele

P.S. Please respond to my correspondence and above all to my offer of help without false modesty and as directly as you are able to. Deliver to me or via your female doctor whenever my daily visit to you proves impossible. Please feel free to share with me whatever weighs heavily on your heart: I think that at the age of thirty-nine one can assess facts and form judgments particularly well, so please have confidence in me just as I have in you. Tell me everything and you will find me a good advisor and for the time being a friend. What happens to us in the future, fate and the future will determine. For now I wait in expectation of a timely answer from you, both willingly and in the hope of hearing from you.

Was this a guardian angel sent to save her? Sabine was very ill, starved, exhausted and wounded in the bombardment. To attract the interest of someone in a position to offer help and protection was a miracle, even if he was German. Perhaps she persuaded herself that, since he was also a prisoner, he couldn't be all bad. Besides, she was also desperate to let her mother know that she was still alive. Being a *Nacht und Nebel* prisoner, she had not been able to receive or send any messages home.

When Gebele wrote his first letter, Sabine had been approximately two to three weeks in Mauthausen. Not long after she was wounded in Amstetten, at the end of March, the British and American armies crossed the Rhine, and there were no further strategic obstacles in their march towards Berlin. The Allied armies moved with great speed: sometimes the front line in Europe moved several kilometers in one day. The Canadian army started its liberation of the still occupied parts of Holland.

On March 13, 1945, Queen Wilhelmina returned, for the first time since 1940, to Holland for a period of ten days. On May 2, she would leave London and return to Holland for good, accompanied by her adjudants, Erik Hazelhoff Roelfzema and Peter Tazelaar.

But in Mauthausen, the war continued for the time being.

Monday,
March 26, 1945

Gebele's second letter is dated March 26, 1945, the day that Amstetten was bombed for the third time in ten days by the Americans. Gebele was still in the *Revier* waiting for an operation on his wounded leg. Sabine had been moved to another *Revier* barrack by now.

In this letter, he thanked Sabine for her reaction to his previous letter in which she apologized for her poorly written German, but Gebele assured her:

> My goodness, liebe Sabine, as far as your mistakes in German are concerned, they are not a problem and even I, as an experienced native German and an academic, make more mistakes than you do and besides, I must tell you, your mistakes are a source of real pleasure, for they have an attractive, childlike naivety for me and therefore there is not the slightest need for apologies.

Gebele begged his "liebe kleine Sabine" to accept his help and reassured her he would do anything he possibly could to lighten her misery. He was convinced of her strength and was sure she would recover. He was confident that the hostilities would end and that she would soon be free.

He seemed to genuinely care for her and promised not to be too overbearing, although, reading this letter, it is difficult to avoid this impression:

> If I may ask a favor, meine liebe Sabine, it would be that you should, for God's sake, avoid all contact with all others in your environment, but for the minimum comradeship of those other women whom fate has destined to be in your situation. [...]
>
> Above all, however, I want to warn you of the danger posed by the male prisoners in the camp, whose craving for sexual favors on a regular basis is too great and quickly leads to disaster.

Sabine should stay strong and pure, he advised. Gebele assured her that he had never had friendships with other prisoners, although he always tried to help wherever he could. Although a little further in the letter, he complained about women in general and the ones in the camp in particular. Time and time again, his kindness was taken advantage of. Most women saw him as a way to leading a life of luxury and damaged his trust. Even in the camp, he had been cheated on and pushed aside by women. Women were disloyal and shameless—he had seen it all in the camp. They even pursued the SS guards in their search for love, "like cows in a meadow constantly searching for fresh grass." According to him, women had inborn bad character traits. But fortunately, he deduced from Sabine's firm and pleasant handwriting a complete absence of these bad traits. In his own words, he himself had only one character fault: jealousy. Although this could also be considered a virtue, because he who is jealous protects his possession and fights for everything that is precious: his beloved.

In this second letter, Gebele already expressed his feelings for her: "Just get better for my sake please and then we shall see what fate will prepare for us. Perhaps love and a future together, perhaps farewell. That I like and love you, liebe Sabine, needs no further mention, though whether you feel the same for me, we shall have to see."

He also asked her to visit him as soon as she was well again: "It would do me good to see you again."

He promised to write to her mother and assured her he would be very discreet. They both knew the punishment would be severe if this were discovered. Almost certainly death.

In order to win her confidence, he told her about his own life.

I am the fourth son of a factory owning married couple, Georg and Franziska Gebele from Munich, where I was born on 12th March 1906.

I studied engineering and despite my considerable youth I made swift progress thanks to my ability. In 1929 I joined Lufthansa as a copilot, but was involved in a serious crash in 1932.

I have been married before and the marriage ended, due to the miserable scheming of my wife, with her death. The marriage produced one child (a girl), who, at the age of fourteen was killed in an air raid on Munich in June 1944.

On Friday, June 9, the Americans had indeed bombed the railway lines around Munich. Five thousand people lost their homes, the roads around the railway station were destroyed, and the hospital was badly damaged. Around 147 people died, including Gebele's daughter. He told Sabine that as a result of shooting his wife for adultery, he was given a three-month suspended sentence. An amazingly light sentence considering. But that was not the reason he was in Mauthausen.

"I also had fourteen previous convictions unfortunately, but thank God, none involved prison or other detentions. They were all fines for traffic offenses and misdemeanors in a car or on a motorcycle. My financial fortunes may not be very important, though I am very well funded and invested in Switzerland, for which I was sentenced to six years in prison on the grounds of currency border offenses, falsification of state documents and similar crimes." Obviously considered more serious than murder by the Nazis.

Looking back on his life as a prisoner, he wondered if he should have done things differently, and on balance thought he should have done so. Perhaps they could discuss it when there was an opportunity to do so in private, he suggested.

Before ending the letter with another declaration of love, he told her he was planning a life abroad after the war and to build a house there, a sort of metaphor for starting a new life.

Sabine must have been pretty shocked at his confessions. To think a man who murdered his wife was now in love with her.

Gebele's state of mind was confused. Sometimes he was formal. Other times he told her his secrets. He tried to win Sabine's confidence by assuring her of his solid financial position and at the same time presented himself as the ideal man. "I don't gamble, I don't drink and I am keen on sports. I also love music and visit the opera often. I am a nature lover. I am also very easygoing and my inclination is to avoid conflicts."

The following day, on Tuesday, March 27, 1945, another letter arrived, starting with "Sabinchen":

Have you received the clothes? Do they fit or should I find different ones for you? The skirt and four blouses I

chose according to my taste and best suited to you. Please,
Sabine, keep them for your own use. For the moment
I have been able only to find underwear for emergency
use. Should you desire something different, Sabinchen,
then your wish is my command and I will see to it.

As a *Funktionshäftling* (a job as part of the authorities in the
camp), he received a daily extra food ration, which he would
happily send on to Sabine.

Furthermore, have you received the bread, sugar and
margarine on Sunday evening? I should like to send you
my everyday garrison special food allowance: something
of substance and nourishing, such as soup, meat and veg-
etables. I don't want to take anyone else into our confidence or bother them with something which will require
negotiation on both sides and create jealousy in others.

He was obviously very keen that she should eat well so that
she would be recovered by the time she left the camp, "hopefully in about four weeks' time, when the war will be over
and we will be able to leave the camp together. If things take
a turn for the worse, don't be alarmed, I'll keep watch over
you like a mother over her child or a treasure hunter over the
most precious jewel he has just unearthed."

Gebele's prediction is eerily prescient. Two days short of
four weeks later, she was indeed liberated.

Sabine was still in the *Revier*, although it might have been
a different one from the one where she met Gebele. He had
made sure that as soon as her ankle improved, she could come
and visit him in his staff quarters. He arranged for her to
be collected and returned to him, so that they could talk

undisturbed about important decisions for the future that might concern them both.

But apart from worrying about Sabine, he had meanwhile also written to Moeder Bien via the Red Cross. He did not mention anything about Sabine's condition in this letter, so as not to worry her mother, other than that she was safe and well.

While reading Gebele's letters, I am torn between feeling grateful that he saved my mother's life, but also fear and oppression when his tone becomes authoritative and demanding. He gets very upset when she does not immediately reply to his letters. "Don't torture me unnecessarily. I feel like a teenager with his first love."

He wanted to know who did her washing and offered to have it done for her. What size shoes did she wear? "I don't want you to be dressed in rags when you leave the camp."

One of his recurring themes is his obsession with her washing. This puzzled me for some time, until I discovered that he was in charge of the laundry as well as being a hospital orderly and working in an office dealing with administration. He was therefore able to provide Sabine with clean clothes (even ironed) and writing paper and pens. The "post" was delivered by the Russian stretcher-bearers who had the freedom of the camp and whom he no doubt had to bribe in some form or other.

The end of the war was now really near. According to news bulletins on the German radio, two-thirds of the country was by now under American occupation.

Wednesday,
March 28, 1945

"Sabine Sonnenschein!"

From this letter, it is clear that Sabine had replied to his letters and that they had seen each other.

> Heartfelt thanks for your charming letter in respect of the package of sugar, bread and margarine.
>
> I have questioned the guilty party and she claims that she had been under the misapprehension that it had been intended for her personally. I have accordingly made my opinion very clear to her and no such misunderstanding will occur again.

Sabine had obviously informed Gebele that she had not received the expected food parcel, and Gebele had immediately found the guilty party. I felt some pity and fear for the poor woman and hope she was not punished in any way.

> Either I shall deliver the items myself or via a reliable messenger or even have the lady doctor pass them you.

I regret my mistake and that you, liebe Sabine, should have been robbed of your provisions through it.

He returned to the subject of her washing and wanted to know if she needed new underwear and to tell him what she "preferred." I feel sure that clothes were not much on her mind while she was still so ill and in pain from her ankle and was desperately trying to stay alive until the end of the war.

She apparently also told him that she trusted him, and Gebele was over the moon. He was now convinced there was a future for them together and wanted to know if she could contemplate being more than friends.

"Sabine, on the subject of the letter to your dear mother, I can today enclose a copy of the letter." He obviously realized that he earned her eternal gratitude by sending this letter to her mother, but I would like to think that he also had some empathy for a mother who did not know if her daughter was dead or alive. I can imagine Moeder Bien would have been elated to receive this letter with its good news.

Gebele was determined to do everything in his power to make Sabine happy, not only while they were in the camp, but if possible, also in the future beyond the camp. He was even prepared to make a "holy vow," which probably meant a marriage.

He was very worried that Sabine had mentioned "work." Overwrought, he wrote: "Liebe kleine Sabine, I am not at all happy that you intend to expose yourself carelessly to danger, running around the camp on a free rein. You will be regarded and possibly treated as fair game and I don't want to see you fall into filthy and lustful hands. You don't know the pitfalls of life in the camp yet." On the other hand, he realized that trying to forbid her anything might have the opposite effect, and he admitted that in the end it would be her decision. But, he wondered, would it not be a better idea if she came to work with him in the office? What did she

think? Working for the big boss, who, like a young boy, was
in love with her?

But it appears that the same day, something unpleasant happened between Gebele and Sabine.

Concerning our conversation today I should like to say
straightaway that I had lost all self control and ask your
forgiveness from the bottom of my heart for forcing myself on you.

It would seem Gebele had tried to kiss her or worse, and
Sabine had rejected him. She was obviously shocked and told
him that his love was not reciprocated with the same intensity. Gebele was upset and wondered if this was because he
was German. Since he had met Sabine, he couldn't think of
anyone else. He couldn't concentrate on anything and was
constantly preoccupied with the thought that she would reject him. He himself was so convinced of his love for her that
he posed her the question, "if you, meine kleine Sabine, will
become my wife?"

They had only known each other for a few days when Gebele wrote his first letter to Sabine. Two days after that, he
tried to kiss her, and the following day, he asked her to marry
him.

Sabine was in a very difficult position. What could she do?
Gebele feared she was indifferent to him, or perhaps the difference in age bothered her. He was thirty-nine, and she was
twenty-six.

When he shares these worries his tone becomes less friendly,
even cross when demanding that she accept his offerings of
food and clothes, "which are strictly for you only." It was
likely that Sabine shared the food that he sent her with her
fellow inmates, and she also told him she did not need any

more clothes. She probably also felt some embarrassment to-wards the other women around her.

Gebele finally ended this long letter with, "It is two o'clock in the morning and I must sleep and dream of you and your future, I shall tell you one day what I have dreamed so far. Waiting for a favorable answer or at least a loving comment…"

I am now reading these letters with a mounting sense of horror, consternation and fear. Was she really in love with Ge-bele as he seemed to think? A few kind words obviously sent him into raptures of happiness and hope. Her position was very difficult. If she offended him, he could send her to the gas chamber, back to do heavy labor, or to the camp brothel. Even if he just abandoned her, her life would be in danger without his protection. She was still very ill and recover-ing from her injuries and broken ankle. Besides, there would be a lot of jealousy from some of the other women over the privileges she received, even though it seemed she was shar-ing them. This was a very dangerous situation as there was a huge air of expectation not only for the war to end any day, but also a pervasion of total lawlessness in the camp. General discipline had slackened considerably.

I can't decide where she was by then—still in the *Revier*, back with the other women in the barrack, or in an alto-gether different place. She clearly still saw her friends, espe-cially Hetty, who had been her bedmate and closest friend throughout this terrible period. The knowledge that he was keeping her alive (and no doubt some of her friends, thanks to the extra rations) was both reassuring and frightening, but by talking about becoming his wife and a future together, he must have shaken her badly. His embarrassment about try-ing to physically take advantage of her sounds sincere. It was probably just a passionate embrace. Most likely she just used him to stay alive, but he confused the gratitude she showed him with love. She had not much choice though. Staying alive was all that mattered.

Meanwhile, Gebele had already told Sabine he would write to her mother, and he enclosed a copy with his letter to her.

Gebele's Letter
to Moeder Bien

25th March 1945

Dear Madame!

With the agreement of your daughter, Sabine Zuur, I permit myself as a stranger to send a few lines in this manner. Your daughter is currently located in the concentration camp in Mauthausen Oberdonau (Austria), having come here well cared for and in good health from Ravensbrück. She is doing well here and if I may tell you this, I will most definitely look after her in an honorable manner, protect her and watch over her. Rest assured, Madame, that my support takes place with honest intentions and my letter to you, dear Madame, occurs at the wish of your daughter, thus there is no reason to be concerned. Miss Zuur is well situated here in an office, her physical care leaves nothing to be desired, her physical condition is good and generally suited to the camp. The transfer of the camp stay from Ravensbrück to here took place due to evacuation before the enemy.

In line with my assigned task, I add the most sincere greetings and best wishes from your daughter, adding that you may most certainly look forward to her return in the near future, and if you would like, then you can, dear Madame, write to your daughter yourself, but without any mention of any kind of my lines written to you today and its more detailed information.

Miss Sabine Zuur, born on 15th July 1918 in Semarang, Dutch East Indies.

Prisoner no. 2851 currently in the concentration camp Mauthausen Oberdonau, Germania.

A letter from a German in a concentration camp? What did Moeder Bien think when she received this letter, or did she even receive it? Unbeknownst to Sabine, her mother had moved several times since she was imprisoned, so her current address was not known to her daughter. As a *Nacht und Nebel* prisoner, Sabine was to all intents and purposes dead. The food parcels that had been sent to her in Ravensbrück never reached her, and the labels were returned as Person Unknown. If she did receive the letter, it must have been a huge relief to hear her daughter was in good health and coping well and above all that she could be expected to return home before too long. But who was this German who was caring for her daughter?

On April 1, 1945, Easter Day, Franz Gebele sent his fifth very long letter to his "liebe Sabine Sonnenschein." They had met up during the day, and Gebele felt "blessed." He had also received a letter from her, which had helped him through a difficult night.

He wondered why Sabine objected to his constant offerings. Would she not have done the same if she were in his place? He saw it as his holy mission to help people in need. Sabine must have wondered why he was only helping her while thousands were dying of hunger and enduring terrible conditions. But for Gebele, no one else compared to his Sabine.

"So stop complaining," he wrote, "about being spoiled because I might get very angry at my Sonnenschein. Do you hear me?"

It sounds like friendly banter, but considering his and her positions in the camp, it also infers a threat. Gebele was getting more and more overwrought, and no one in the camp—not the *Kapos* (prisoners who worked for and with the Germans) or other prisoners or perhaps especially him, could be relied on or trusted. From an emotionally damaged Gebele, such a threat could be very serious.

Sabine's ankle was still very painful, and Gebele had asked the doctor for advice, but according to him, the pain was part of the healing process. "In the beginning," he said, "when trying to walk, pain is normal, especially in the groin and swollen glands, and around the break." But despite this reassurance, Gebele had asked him to inspect Sabine's ankle the following day. He could then also make sure there were no other health problems.

Keep strong, Sabine, don't be afraid. I watch over you. You are not alone in the camp.

Gebele was pressing for an answer to his important question (of marrying him), and Sabine had promised an answer once she had returned home. But Gebele struggled to accept this. He couldn't wait. It was keeping him awake at night, but he also realized that too much pressure on her might have the opposite effect. He therefore begged her not to tell him if she decided against it. He would rather not know, but if she agreed, she could tell him straightaway.

Sabine by now felt confident enough to ask Gebele if he could help the woman in the bed next to her, and he promised to ask the doctor to attend to her as well. So at this stage, she was clearly still in the *Revier*.

But other news had reached Sabine. Her friend Dr. Steijns had also arrived in Mauthausen. Despite there being tens of thousands of prisoners, news of anyone from home arriving would spread like wildfire through the camp. Sabine had been a patient of Michel (Chel) Steijns before the war, and his wife, Grace, had been one of the women delivering food parcels and toiletries when she was in the Utrecht jail. Chel had been arrested for his illegal activities shortly after Sabine was in Utrecht, and he had now also arrived in Mauthausen via Camp Vught, Bergen-Belsen and Dachau, more dead than alive. Because of his appalling physical condition, he had been put in the *Totenlager*, the barrack where the dying were left to die. The *Totenlager* was situated outside the camp near the granite quarry, the Wiener Graben.

As soon as she heard the news about him, she asked Gebele if he could save Dr. Steijns, and this request most certainly did save his life.

Gebele at first told her he had tried to find Dr. Steijns, but so far had not succeeded. He asked if she could find out where in the camp he might be, and he would ask the doctor to visit him. He was only too happy to help a compatriot of Sabine, even though it was at great risk to himself. He already found out that Dr. Steijns had several times suffered serious punishments and was known to the SS. "Because your friend has been sent to the punishment bunker several times both here and in Vught, he is being watched carefully." But despite that, Gebele promised her that he would do all he could to help him and would keep Sabine informed.

He warned her to never make a list of names "for your own and all your Dutch friends' safety. If it would be discovered during an inspection it could have serious consequences and result in many deaths."

It is likely that Gebele, like many high-ranking officers in the camp, listened to BBC radio to keep abreast of the developments at the Front, as German radio did not give this information. He seemed well-informed of what was going on.

He impressed on Sabine not to lose heart, because the war would end soon and "our friends are already within twenty kilometers of Vienna."

In his previous letters, he referred to the Allies as the enemy, when they conquered Bavaria, but now they were "friends." He reassured her that Mauthausen would very shortly be liberated. Vienna was about 200 km to the east and Bavaria less than 150 km to the west of the camp. He tried to prepare Sabine for the liberation and told her to start collecting her belongings, so that when the time came, he would collect "meine liebe Sabine" and take her to safety. He finished with best wishes and added a postscript: "Is your underwear in the laundry? Were the clothes okay?"

While Gebele's obsessive care is oppressive and feels like she is his hostage, it is also reassuring to read that he tried so hard to protect and help her.

During these last few days, while he was fussing over her broken ankle and her poor state of health, a deadly typhoid epidemic was devastating the camp. While many others succumbed through exhaustion, were shot dead or were sent to the gas chambers, so near liberation, Sabine and her close friends seem to have been fairly safe thanks to Gebele.

Wednesday,
April 4, 1945

Gebele was working overtime and often wrote to Sabine in the middle of the night.

On this Wednesday, April 4, he wrote at 2 a.m. and told her he had only just returned from work. It is not clear where he was living, but it is likely that he slept where he worked.

He had received a "sweet" letter from Sabine, for which he thanked her, although he was surprised by the content. She had told him that the rumor going around was that prisoners would be freed very shortly. Gebele confirmed that there was a possibility, or rather, there had been a discussion about an exchange of prisoners of certain nationalities, the Dutch, Danish and Norwegians. This would not happen immediately because the Red Cross in Geneva and the Swiss government were still in negotiations (with Himmler), and there was still uncertainty over the outcome. Gebele announced he was involved in this process and was working on a document relating to it. Or so he said.

"I am happy that you will all be free soon." According to Gebele, the lists with names of the possible male and female evacuees from these countries had been compiled that very day, and included "a certain little Sabine Zuur."

Gebele, elated that he could make sure Sabine would be on this list, was prepared to work all night. The camp authorities were very keen to make this plan work, thinking the Allies would see them in a better light if they agreed to these exchanges. They thought the same goodwill would be returned if they built a "*neues Revier*" (a new hospital), showing off their good care of the prisoners. According to Gebele, "They are scared witless of the consequences for them personally. They are simply trying to rescue their reputations, these criminals." Gebele wrote what was for him a rather bald statement about his superiors.

Meanwhile, Sabine had written to him to say how sorry she was that they would be separated so shortly after they had gotten to know each other and that she feared he would soon forget her. But Gebele assured her, "I know that your departure will hit me hard and that, perhaps at the key moment I may behave in a somewhat unmanly fashion from a mixture of joy and tearful pain…only the future and fate will reveal to us what is to become of me and then I shall be pleased to resume our correspondence and indeed come to visit you, but only if you feel for me more than friendship."

He continued for many pages declaring his love like a teenager, until he came to his senses and announced he must stop thinking about her departure or "otherwise I will still be here tomorrow night."

However, he still reminisced also about the day of his arrest, August 20, 1936: "I know that I am forty years old and 'unfortunately' German. My degree qualification and doctorate were revoked by the People's Court of Justice on August 20th 1936 on the basis of my conviction. I cannot and will not return to life in this unjustly based German social structure from which I have been ejected merely because I sought to bring to safety human beings who had been persecuted and robbed and plundered down to the last penny of their savings, just for the benefit of the masses. At the high point of my life I was forced to sacrifice my future to the ignominy of a regime and their crimes, in order to finally end up loveless and dishonored in a concentration camp, branded a criminal."

Where in the outside world would he find a woman who would understand what he had suffered, "but you, Sabine, you understand what it is to drain the poisoned chalice." Like him, she had endured terrible hardship and had been a witness to mass annihilation. He longed for a woman who had shared his hardships, who was not frightened by the horror stories of the hell he had lived in. Their shared experiences would form an eternal bond.

> Yes, I love you with the last drop of my blood and I beg you to tell me one thing, in case we may not meet again. If you really understand how I feel, will you please give me your hand in marriage?

He confessed that if he had not had his daughter, he would probably have ended his life years ago. Now that the war was nearing its end, there was another challenge waiting for him: life in freedom. Even so, he had already made plans.

He would move to Valencia and start a business, something to do with cars or planes, a typewriter shop or something where he could use his professional qualification as an engineer. He had even already written to certain persons abroad, although he was aware that, after this disastrous war, the Germans would be vilified everywhere in the world. But he would manage. The thought of freedom encouraged him to think about a new life away from Germany, with a soul mate, to start a new business, to build a house and have children.

Unfortunately I was not able to come and see you yesterday evening, as the gate was locked until the Hauptsturmführer appeared. I had such a good supper prepared for you, but had to retreat without reaching you. Your washing is being completed today, Thursday, and will be ironed tomorrow. I have an appointment with Dr. Steijns today and he sends greetings to you via my adjudant.

Meanwhile it is 4 a.m. and I can no longer function properly. Tiredness and pain summon me to stop. What is on my tongue I can no longer say.

If the issue of your release suddenly becomes imminent, please send Nadja to call me immediately and if we don't see each other again, meine liebe Sonnenschein, please always remember, there is someone who loves you from the bottom of his heart, you little Seelchen, and will remain loyal to you, waiting, free from all sadness, for a single word. A man to whose life you gave meaning.

From this long letter, it is clear that Gebele was nearly succumbing to stress. He was hardly able to put his words together coherently. The situation in the camp was becoming more chaotic by the day, despite the end of the war inexorably nearing. The transports taking their victims to the gas chambers increased, and the desperation of the regime to hide their barbaric deeds intensified. People, administration, everything was being destroyed as quickly as possible.

Reading Gebele's letters, I begin to feel more and more suffocated. Sabine must have felt that ten times over. She couldn't reject him because she needed his help and protection, and above all, she depended on him to put her name on the evacuation list.

With Gebele's increasing insistence for an answer to his big question (would she marry him), Sabine's anxiety must also have intensified. She could not rebuff him too much as she needed him to survive. Apart from that, with any luck, he might have placed her at the top of his evacuation list.

In March 1945, Count Folke Bernadotte, on behalf of the Red Cross, started negotiations with the Nazis from neutral Sweden, regarding the liberation and evacuation of concentration camp prisoners. Bernadotte was a member of the Swedish royal family and possessed an enormous and influential network. His opposite partner was Heinrich Himmler, who, unlike Hitler himself, still saw possibilities to save the German Reich. For Himmler, freeing prisoners was not a humanitarian question, but rather an effort to save what was left of his country, not to mention his own skin.

His problem was that in order to agree to evacuations, he had to allow the Red Cross entry to the camps, without them somehow discovering what barbarities had been committed there. The negotiations dragged on and on, but Bernadotte did not give up. He had already succeeded in freeing Norwegian and Danish prisoners at an earlier stage, while the Red Cross had sat on its hands and had done nothing to free prisoners.

Talks between Bernadotte and Himmler took place, among others, in Hohenlychen, just 10 km from Ravensbrück. But even when evacuations had been agreed to, it was difficult to put them into practice. To drive convoys of seriously ill, wounded and traumatized people through a Europe ravaged by war and still fighting was a nearly impossible feat.

Nevertheless, between March 16 and May 1, 1945, Bernadotte managed to save 15,000 people. On April 2, a convoy of white buses departed for the German/Austrian border to collect prisoners from Dachau and Mauthausen. From the Danish border, this was a journey of more than 1,000 km. In Mauthausen, they collected sixteen *Nacht und Nebel* women, all

Scandinavian. Sabine was not among them. Did Gebele try to get her on this convoy, or could he not bear to part with her?

Sabine must have felt destroyed. I found a short letter that Gebele sent her the same day:

> Meine liebling, you go on to say that you are not con-
> cerned by the thought of a possible evacuation. I am
> afraid such an attitude ought to make me really angry
> with you. Are you aware what effect statements like that
> have on me? I hardly imagine you can, otherwise you
> would not write such things to me. I can only hope you
> don't seriously mean it.

But for Sabine, it made no difference whether the whole camp was liberated by the Allies or whether the Red Cross took only a group of people. As long as she could leave.

Gebele had of course realized that if his Sonnenschein left Mauthausen, he would be left on his own. For him life only had meaning if "his" Sabine was there too.

Thursday,
April 5, 1945

Gebele at last managed to visit Dr. Steijns. He was horrified
to find him in such a miserable condition. Not only physically, but mentally too. Dr. Steijns had been forced to treat the
sick in the *Totenlager*, which was down in the Wiener Graben.
Since there was no equipment or medicine available, it was,
in reality, impossible to treat patients. For a doctor, this must
have been an added agony to his own failing health.

"I have assured him of my complete support," Gebele wrote,
"and I am making sure he can leave here [the *Totenlager*] and
that he will have a better place to work and have better food."

Gebele was impressed by Dr. Steijns's demeanor and was
convinced he was a good doctor and a sensitive man. He was
also touched by Dr. Steijns's honesty in relating what he had
suffered in Camp Vught. Gebele was not used to people taking
him into their confidence, and he accepted the doctor as "a
true comrade whom I have saved out of the clutches of death."

He also passed grateful thanks from Dr. Steijns to Sabine
for worrying about him.

Just as Gebele had sent a letter to Sabine's mother to reassure her, he now sent a letter to Dr. Steijns's wife to tell her that her husband was alive. He promised he would give Sabine more details about Dr. Steijns when she next came to visit him in his office.

Friday,
April 6, 1945

Mein kleiner Sabine-liebling,

I learned with great joy this afternoon that the expected conference came to a decision in your favor and that you all will get home via the Swedish Red Cross. For me this means that today is a day of greater happiness than I have experienced in the camp or indeed at all over the last eleven years. My angel Sabine is going home and although I deplore the fact, I in no way regret wishing you from the bottom of my heart all the very best for your journey and your arrival in your homeland.

I ask for your forgiveness therefore if you, poor little Sabine, were hungry and the stupid big boy failed at the decisive moment to provide you with anything to eat. I will do my best to deliver something tasty and for the last time look into your lovely eyes.

Gebele was struggling with the idea of losing Sabine so shortly after he had fallen in love with her. He told her he had never loved anyone like he loved her. As soon as possible after the war, he wanted to visit her in Holland and get married. Then he would take mother and daughter to a home of their own. If necessary, he would renounce his nationality and become a Dutch national. He also suggested that, as soon as she was home, she should check the newspapers on the first, tenth and twentieth of the month. He planned to set up a public search message so that they could quickly reestablish contact and "she will have her big boy with her soon enough." Sabine could count on him to sort out his affairs at home after the end of the war, and within a month, "you will hear from me."

> And now, my Seelchen, please greet your dear mum (although she does not know me), from the bottom of my heart. It will be a great joy for me to be allowed to get to know her and value her and, perhaps, (somewhat too bold and premature) also be allowed to greet her as "Mams."

It seems Gebele had lost all sense of reality by now. He did not seem to realize that Moeder Bien most likely would not have wanted to meet him at all.

He also informed Sabine that her plaster cast would be removed the next day and that perhaps there would be an opportunity to meet and say a few important words.

He admitted to being so overjoyed that he was struggling to be coherent in this letter and also asked for a small memento of her. A lock of hair, perhaps?

"Concerning your request about your friend from Ravensbrück, I will keep you informed via a messenger." This referred to Hetty. Sabine must have asked Gebele to put her on the same transport list.

Gebele had managed not only to get Dr. Steijns away from the Wiener Graben, but also to get his name on the evacuation list, while daily hundreds were still being murdered. Dr.

Steijns would be put on either her transport or the second one, which would leave for Switzerland on April 15. How Gebele managed this feat is difficult to understand. He was a prisoner himself, although he had an official job and therefore some influence. But did he falsify papers or manage to persuade his superiors, or was some bribery involved?

Dr. Steijns's health, once removed from the *Totenlager* and no longer having to work, started to improve slowly under the care of another doctor.

Gebele had taken Dr. Steijns into his confidence about his love for Sabine and even let him read her letters. He apologized, but assured her that the doctor enjoyed their love for each other.

Gebele and Sabine had not seen each other for a few days, but via a third person, Gebele had found out exactly where Sabine's bed was located. Gebele assured her he would recognize his liebe Sabine Sonnenschein immediately among all the other women.

According to Gebele, his contact with Sabine made him the envy of his superiors. They thought he would have a happy future with her once they were married. "Two honest hearts have found each other," they said.

By now the situation in the camp was lawless and dangerous, and Gebele warned her that she had to be careful with whom she spent time, especially Germans. There were spies everywhere among the prisoners. He warned her to think about their future.

Some more teasing lines followed, which again suggest an implied threat rather than a joke:

As regards to you: don't think that you can avoid the punishment I have condemned you to. No, no! Even though you assume I will not kiss you in the presence of

the other women, I cannot promise that. You are by now
so in arrears of punishments, that I cannot wait any longer. Just you wait, mein liebling…

Dr. Steijns also sent her a letter on that same day. It is an
emotional letter in pencil, thanking Sabine for saving his life.

Friday
Dear friend!
Thanks to your kind heart, which did not forget what
Dr. S. did for his patients in Vught, and through the influence and power of Mr. Gebele, I was suddenly transferred yesterday from block 4, where I was suffering
a very high temperature for the last week (no known
cause), to the *Häftlingsrevier* [prisoners' hospital]. The
difference is as night and day. My hope for the future
is restored. I am confident I will see my wife and child
again and resume my work. I cannot express my feelings
enough. Many, many thanks! For the time being I am in
room 19, but Mr. G has promised me that from Monday
I will be in room 13. Lovely and quiet.

I am ashamed when I think of the conditions you
poor women suffer. Mr. G showed me your description
of them. How can you survive this? I long for spring, the
future, so strongly it is nearly unbearable. I dream of the
blossom, the beautiful fields, blue water…

My poor wife who has worked her fingers to the bone
in a far too busy practice. And Niekie, my little daughter,
who really needs the support of her father. Let us hope
and pray that by summer we will be in Holland again and
that the world will be free of this inhuman slaughter…

Now the man who was still so young and energetic
in Vught has shrunk to a poor old Muselmann, who is

ashamed to be seen. [The word *Muselmann* was Jewish
slang used in the camps to refer to inmates who were
near death from starvation, exhaustion and despair. A
person who had reached this stage had little if any chance
of survival.]

I hope when we meet on Monday, that you will have
read this and take pity on a once so vain man, whose own
wife said that he was the most arrogant man in Utrecht.

You of course have not changed. You were always
courageous and tremendously optimistic, but for you too,
without doubt, the suffering of others will be the heavi-
est. What happened in the lager down below, I would
not have survived much longer...

Let's hope that we will both be healthy when we make
the return to our lovely kind country together, where you
will meet the kindest woman in Utrecht (my wife) and
who will receive you like no other has ever been received.

I do not ask you to write to me in return, because I
realize this would be difficult for you, but may I write
to you again?
Steijns

He later sent her a short note to impress on her to exercise
her foot, in view of the expected evacuation.

Dear Sabine,
From your old doctor some good advice: exercise, exercise. Think of all the possibilities. It will be painful, very
painful to begin with, but every day is progress and your
general state of health is now good enough to be prepared
for anything that may happen. Remember and follow
my advice, like in the past. Do you promise, my girl?
Bye, your Steijns

Gebele also encouraged Sabine to eat well and exercise her ankle. It seems she was both physically and mentally in a bad place at this stage, still very ill and no doubt feeling very depressed. Perhaps she was not helped by the obsessive and insistent letters from Gebele. Whereas he saw her as a symbol of hope, she perhaps felt despair when seeing him. The end of the war was so near—Sabine knew that too—but every day waiting must have seemed endless.

Gebele, however, was still preoccupied with her well-being, as is obvious from a note he sent her with a parcel of food: semolina, sugar, noodles, sausage, dried onion, margarine, oats, spices and biscuits. For the next day he promised milk, pudding, eggs, flour and raspberry juice, enclosing a note: "I wish you a good appetite. Your Franz."

Sunday,
April 8, 1945

Gebele was still very busy, but he nevertheless found time to read Sabine's letters to him and to reply to them. His days were very long. Sometimes he worked until after midnight and then began a long letter to Sabine, before starting work again at the crack of dawn. There was not much time for sleep, although he admitted he sometimes took a nap at lunchtime when work was finished. He knew it was not good for his own health, but for Sabine he was prepared to give up his sleep.

On this day, he was writing his letter outside in the sunshine and hoped she would also be outside when she wrote to him. The sunshine might give her freckles. He was glad Hetty was sitting next to her, writing out recipes during her last letter to him. This was considered a good way to occupy your mind and stop feeling hungry.

Gebele's work consisted of piles of papers to do with the foreign detainees, but they would have to wait. Today Sabine was Gebele's priority.

On the following day, Monday, April 9, all German nationals in the camp, as well as Spaniards, East Europeans,

Poles and Sudeten Germans, would have to get ready to depart for Innsbruck, where they would be deployed as personnel, meaning, to act as guards for other prisoners evacuated from Mauthausen.

The evacuation was slowly getting nearer, Gebele said, since "our friends," meaning the Allies, had already occupied Vienna and the surrounding areas.

The Russians were also approaching rapidly from the opposite direction. "The east Front is not going well," Gebele wrote. Like the SS, he was very afraid to fall into Russian hands. Their reputation regarding their treatment of Germans went before them.

> There were large transports in the last twenty-four hours. Some 16,500 people have arrived and are ready to depart again if the order comes. I am worried about you, my darling, because if things start to move, you may be stuck here, despite my efforts. But do not fear. I will make sure that I will stay behind with you if this turns out to be the case.

Gebele was worried about not only Sabine's fate, but also his own. He wondered what the future held for him. Many problems, he feared. It would be bittersweet if a man of thirty-nine would have to give up hope and depend on pity and help from others. No, he was determined to manage. He could say, without boasting too much, that before his arrest, he had been a successful man. His colleagues had even spoken of a degree of genius in his achievements. "I have always achieved my goals and have never given up, in my professional life, nor while in uniform, or on a personal or emotional level. I always strived to reach my goal and have always been successful."

Meanwhile, Gebele had taken steps to proceed with his plans to start up his dream business. He said he had entered negotiations via a Swiss firm to become a dealer of American cars. All in deepest secret, of course. In addition to that, he was researching an exclusive agency for typewriters and office equipment in Seville. He even had a written contract already, but of course it could be difficult for him, as a "bad German," to do this sort of job, although, considering his excellent references from before the war, there should not be too many problems.

> This brings me to a question directly relating to you, meine liebe Sabine. One I have asked you before, but which, so far, you have not replied to. Would you be prepared to act as my company chairman in such a business?

Considering the circumstances, this seems a premature request. Sabine's sole preoccupation was how to survive the camp. Of course, another question is hidden in the first, the "big" question to which she had up until now not given him an answer: Was she prepared (with her mother too) to start a new life with him in another country?

This question preoccupied Gebele's thoughts continuously, and her silence on the matter caused him great anxiety. Sabine had admitted that the relationship between them would have been very different if they had had some time to get to know each other, and Gebele did agree that with the lack of privacy and time, it was a problem that stopped them from surrendering to their feelings and longing for intimacy with each other. They were constantly surrounded by others.

He suggested he would make sure that during her next visit to him, they would be alone, hoping his secret wishes would be fulfilled, although he promised her that nothing would happen that she did not want to happen. "You cannot imagine what pain it would cause me to do something against your will."

Sabine had replied that she couldn't help that he was tortured by his desire for her. Although she had made clear to him that she trusted him and wanted to see him happy, she was not in love with him. It seemed unrealistic to her to form a lifelong bond that was based on an unequal partnership. She would find it difficult to leave him behind when she could finally leave herself, and it would be easy to give him his desired answer, but she could not bring herself to do so, although she had promised she would always think about him and she would look forward to a visit from him. But for Gebele, this was not enough—he literally dreamed of walking her down the aisle: "I held you in my arms at the Lido in Italy. We were on honeymoon and you were so in love with me. We were both so happy. Can this not become reality? I asked the flowers and they said: yes. I asked the stars and they said: yes."

Gebele had already explained to Sabine how he would try and trace her via the newspapers, and he now also told her that he would ask communal friends there (did he mean Hetty and Dr. Steijns?) to put in a good word for him with Sabine and invite them to their wedding.

And if she still refused to say yes, then punishment would be "unavoidable." He added, "You will feel very uncomfortable if I have to ask my German friends here to put in a good word for me with you. It is easier for you to say 'yes' now." Did he mean his superiors? It was said supposedly in jest, but sounds more like a threat.

Dr. Steijns was also aware of the intrusive behavior of the man who saved his life and even dared to comment on it, but Gebele fended off his comment with another "joke":

Doctor Steijns is here with me at the moment and he sends you his warm greetings. He hopes to see you again before long. He will personally make contact with you. He accuses me of trying to overwhelm you and wants you to be the judge in this affair. I therefore ask you, at this stage of the proceedings, to be lenient with me and award me a light sentence, Miss "Strafhof." If you sentence me to a lifelong marriage to a certain Sabine Zuur from The Hague, I will confess my guilt and accept the punishment you mete out for the rest of my life.

The juggling act Sabine had to manage was getting more and more arduous as the end of the war was getting nearer and nearer. Despite his assurances that he did not want to put any pressure on Sabine, Gebele was becoming more desperate by the day at the thought of losing Sabine forever once she left the camp.

Sabine felt responsible for Hetty and Dr. Steijns, and the last thing she wanted to risk was putting not only her own life but also theirs in danger by rejecting Gebele.

Monday,
April 9, 1945

The letter Sabine received from Gebele this Monday, in reply to her letter to him the previous evening, was, by his standards, very short, and must have been a shock for Sabine:

> Seelchen, something very different for now. You will all be sent to the Wiener Graben barracks. Tomorrow the beds will arrive. I will try and do my utmost best to help you in any way I can. I will not abandon you.
>
> Today I should have joined the SS, but because of you I have managed to avoid doing so in order to keep supporting you and work in the general interest of others. I find it impossible to leave you in adversity by yourself.
>
> I also ask your permission to collect your lock of hair and my Easter present in person. To be more precise the last one I will receive personally, the lock of hair you can enclose in your next letter please. As always dirty washing to me. And please reply to my last question regarding your provisional "yes" to my marriage proposal. Can I

look on you as my little bride until you return home and
will you in return consider me your faithful bridegroom
(until we are reunited)? Please give me a reply along with
all your love. Give me your heart, your future. I will also
keep my word to you, in faithful affection and loyalty.
With best wishes and a big kiss, your Franz

According to Gebele, around 1,600 women were to be
taken down to the barracks in the Wiener Graben, of whom
Sabine was one. The barracks turned out to be several big open
sheds with straw on the floor. In order to stop any revolt by
the prisoners, the SS operated a divide-and-rule system and
appointed prisoners, such as prostitutes and Roma women, as
the people in charge. To make sure they did not to lose this
privilege, the women were more than prepared to hand out
harsh punishments to their fellow prisoners. They ran a cruel
regime, making the miserable lives of their charges even more
unbearable. The Roma and prostitutes were likely hardened
due to their lowly place in society, and this was a chance for
them to take revenge on the very women who had always
treated them as outcasts. The Germans knew they would run
a brutal regime and offer little sympathy to the prisoners.

I have long been wondering what the Easter present to be
"collected in person" that Gebele refers to could have been.
What or how could she organize any present for him?

Could he be referring to his much desired intimacy that Sabine vaguely had promised in the future? Or was it just her promise to marry him that he wanted to hear in person? It seemed
impossible for her to keep him at a distance for much longer.

She did write him a letter in which she finally professed
her love for him. Gebele was beside himself with happiness.
"Sabine, Seelchen, I am so happy. Seelchen, you tell me you
love me. You have no idea how happy your big boy now feels."

Liberation was so near, and yet the following day, Sabine, with the other women, were be moved down to the Wiener Graben, the hellhole down below the camp.

I can imagine she must have felt almost paralyzed with fear that Gebele, her only hope for survival, was in danger of being sent to the Front. The situation in the camp had become so desperate that all civilian personnel, police and soldiers were forced to enter the SS, the organization that had been ordered by Himmler himself to run and guard the camps and commit murder on a grand scale. Nine hundred German nationals in the camp were forced to sign up, but Gebele managed to avoid being recruited. "I love you, I will not leave your side, because it is safer if I am close to you in case you need help."

Mauthausen was one of the last camps to be liberated. Camp Commandant Ziereis was determined to leave as little evidence as possible for the Allies to find about the terrible treatment of his prisoners. As the Front approached, he forced prisoners to leave the camp on foot to no one knew where in order not to fall into the hands of the liberators. Those unable to walk, in fact anyone who stayed behind, would be murdered. Although, all the time, behind Hitler's back, Himmler was still negotiating with the Red Cross to evacuate groups of prisoners and cooperate with the Allies to save himself, knowing that Germany was losing the war.

By now many concentration camps, including many of the subcamps around Mauthausen, had already been liberated by the Allies, causing the numbers in Mauthausen to swell by thousands of prisoners sent on from other camps, especially from Eastern Europe. The surplus prisoners were packed in wherever there was a space, in the quarry, in improvised tents or just anywhere. Their suffering was unimaginable.

Tuesday,
April 10, 1945

By the second week of April, the camp authorities were desperate. They no longer received orders from Berlin, as usual, or if they came, they were contradictory. On the one hand, no prisoners were allowed to fall into Allied hands, so the killing intensified. On the other hand, there were still ongoing negotiations with the Red Cross. Many of the guards who had worked in the camp had deserted. The situation within the camp was always dire, but in the last few weeks of the war, it deteriorated alarmingly.

When Sabine met Gebele for the first time, he was still wearing the striped prison uniform, but by now, being pressed into a more official role, he was wearing an army uniform, perhaps even an SS uniform.

He himself had not joined the SS, as he was just a prisoner with privileges, but with the situation deteriorating, it was a case of all hands on deck. Despite his criminal past, his superiors obviously had enough confidence in him to put him on watch at the entrance gate.

This Tuesday, at 2 a.m., Gebele wrote to Sabine in response to a letter she had sent him, and they had also managed to meet in person that day. It seems Sabine had finally given in to his pressure of marriage, and Gebele was over the moon with the "engagement." He felt young again and wrote, "Now I know you really love me from the bottom of your heart and I will be forever grateful. I will remember this to my dying day."

Although elated, he felt sad at the same time because the evacuation plan had failed. That same evening, the Swiss Red Cross had decided that it would be too great a risk to evacuate the Dutch. The announcement on the radio at nine o'clock the night before had said that the delegation from the Red Cross had been unable to find a way through to the camp. "This means that there is no way you will be leaving... All of this is a source of great sadness, because it not only concerns you, but also Dr. Steijns and many of your male and female compatriots. I would like to put a bomb underneath all these incompetents."

Meanwhile he kept reminding her to practice her walking, so that in the event of an emergency, she could save herself. She could trust him never to abandon her, and he would do everything in his power to help her. He would stay in the camp as long as Sabine was still there.

Gebele had passed on Sabine's greetings to Dr. Steijns, and he in return sent his greetings back to her. He too was bitterly disappointed about the failed evacuation plans.

Dr. Steijns is as depressed about the news as I am, but he says we must not give up hope. To be honest he is in a deplorable state, but I can't bring myself to tell him that.

I do wonder if he will make it. It would be such a pity. He is a good friend and an honest man. He always cheers up when I talk about you and tells me that he cannot think of a more loving man for his little Zuurtje than me (he orders me to tell you this).

Sabine had expressed her concern about Gebele's refusal to join the SS, but he reassured her again, "Don't worry, your big boy knows what to do and what to avoid." He explained again that he did not want to join the SS because, first, he wanted to stay in the camp while she was still there, and second, he hated the regime. His only preoccupation was to leave with Sabine and go to Holland now, knowing that his little Sonnenschein was all his.

He looked forward to meeting her mother and hoped they could live with her until they were married. "I hope she will like me and accept me as her extra son." Sabine had told him that her mother would never want to live with one of her children, plus spouse. This was incomprehensible to Gebele, and he did not agree. "She has to come and live with us. But there is no point fighting about it at this stage. We shall see who wins when the time comes, you, me or your mother."

Even though he had known Sabine for only a few weeks, this did not stop him making big plans for the future:

You once told me you would like to have children and this is the reason why Mum should live with us: because of the children. Not as a nanny, but to enjoy them. I would love it if she could share our love and happiness and, in the last chapter of her life live happily with us. Look, Sabine, the spring and summer of her life have passed and autumn is about to begin. Should she now be lonely and alone? No, she belongs with her children and grandchildren, that is my holy aim.

This reminded him that so far, she had told him little about her family. What sort of job did her father and brothers have before the war? He was really interested, but Sabine did not give him much information. "Just you wait, naughty girl. When I come down below with the Professor on Friday to see how you are. Punishment is unavoidable and I will kiss your lips so intensely that you will need treatment from the Professor. So, please reply to some of my questions in your next letter, okay?"

This was another of his little teasing jokes, but considering Sabine's circumstances, it sounded more like an implied threat. He fantasized, when the opportunity arose, about taking one of his superiors' cars, driving through Switzerland and spending a few days together in Munich on their way to Holland. But it seemed they would first have to finish drinking the poisoned chalice "before we are free to do as we like." He meant the failed evacuation to Switzerland, although he was convinced it would still happen within the next few days. The news from the Front was hopeful.

The letter writing was a risky business. And keeping the letters even more so. Despite this, Gebele asked Sabine to keep his letters and hoped she would take them home with her. They were his holy symbols of his love for her:

Sabine, my angel, I have to tell you one thing. Once home, when it is known that we are engaged, I do not want to wait too long to get married. For my part, our "abreigung" [engagement] does not need to be long, or do you object? Hmm. Kleine Sabine, please don't object.

Sabine must have felt absolutely desperate and depressed. Twice now the evacuation had not happened. Liberation was so near and yet so far. She had been forced to give in to

Gebele's constant demands for an engagement and her declarations of love. Of course, she was eternally grateful for everything he did for her, but marrying him and taking him to Holland? It was a total fantasy, although Gebele was utterly convinced. It seemed, as the days went by and the tension rose, that he was losing any sense of reality. It seemed he forgot he was a German oppressor in a concentration camp. And that prisoner or not, he would still be reviled. He clung to the thought of a happy future.

Wednesday,
April 11, 1945

This was the day Buchenwald Concentration Camp was liberated, and Gebele wrote:

Mein kleiner Liebling! Sabine Sonnenschein!...
I heard that the living conditions are unbearable down below and I beg you, my Seelchen, take care with everything you do or touch. Do everything to avoid a last-minute infection. Together with this letter I send you some food and a set of clothes, I hope to your liking. Did the camp secretary hand you the parcels himself? And yesterday the washing and the shoes? I managed to find you a suitcase and ask you to put all your belongings in it.

Today I received a sad postcard with a message that my country house in Prien am Chiemsee has been subjected to an arson attack. It is heavily damaged. My anger is not for the perpetrators, but for the catastrophic powers that be, who make this sort of thing possible. On the other hand, my dear Seelchen, I can manage without my country house, since I have everything I need and, above all, I have you.

Today I also received a strange love letter from a young lady—such overtures from a woman to a man make me want to laugh. It really is shameless.

She wrote that she had heard from other girls and had seen with her own eyes, that I was in the habit of supporting you women wherever I could. She started by asking for food and ended with offering me her love in return.

Tell me, Sabine, are there more such unscrupulous individuals among you? I can't understand it. In this case it concerned a German woman…(I won't tell you what I thought about her).

Can I expect tomorrow or even today some more post from my little darling? Please write as soon as possible.

In the hope that a long letter detailing your needs and wishes will reach me soon, I leave you with best wishes and a thousand passionate kisses.

Your dear big boy, Franz

Thursday,
April 12, 1945

At 10 p.m. this Thursday evening, Gebele wrote to Sabine to tell her that he had received her sweet letter from two days ago, but had not had the time to reply until now. He sent best wishes from Dr. Steijns, whose health continued to improve, as his "towering hunger" proved.

Sabine had relayed to Gebele how bad the situation in the Wiener Graben was, and he told her that some women were due to be moved back to the main camp a few days ago, but somehow this had not happened so far. It was therefore imperative that she kept on with her exercises. The plaster cast was due to be removed, and she must keep on trying to stand and walk.

> Follow mine and the Professor's advice and be brave, my darling. Chin up and keep going. We have to make sure that in case of an evacuation or unforeseen disaster, you can save yourself. The plaster could be a great obstacle.
> In two days' time we will all come down to keep you

company and then punishment for disobedience will take place, love of my life.

Although the women were not removed from the quarry, some improvements were made, sanitation was cleaned up, and those with infectious diseases were separated by wooden partitions from the others. Emergency measures that were unsustainable, according to Gebele.

Sabine complained how badly the Roma women were treating her and the others. After the war, she recalled that they were mostly prostitutes, put in charge by the SS as *Kapos*.

"They enjoyed and used their powerful status as much as they could… As soon as you try to have a moment's rest, one of them will tell you to go back to work. They don't give you a moment's peace." These barracks were also called the "*Zigeuner Baracke*" (the barracks where the Roma women were kept). According to eyewitnesses, the thirty or so barracks down in the quarry were little more than damp, drafty wooden huts without glass in the windows. Of course, the other reason it was so awful to be there was the direct view onto the gruesome *Todesstiege* (death stairs).

Yes, Seelchen, this infamous death staircase has cost thousands their lives and is the symbol for Camp Mauthausen. Many a prominent member of society who no doubt never expected to end his life that way has perished on it. You write that you were in tears at the sight of it, but, my dear Seelchen, do not cry. Be brave. This is just one more lesson in the school of life that you will have to learn in order to become hard as steel.

She had to get through this to be able to start a new life with him, he told her. "Bravery and humor will help you through this despair and misery."

The valley where the barracks are is dominated on one side by the steep wall of the quarry and the horrendous spectacle of the stairs going up the side, but on the other side, beautiful countryside can be glimpsed through the barbed wire fencing.

Sabine wrote to Gebele that the sight of the spring flowers made her very homesick; according to Gebele, no one could be unmoved seeing this idyllic landscape around them, "only those who have lost their moral compass."

While writing this long letter, Gebele suddenly found himself in the dark. The electricity had been turned off, and he had to continue by candlelight. He was convinced it wouldn't be long before they would be reunited forever. She had no idea how hot-blooded he was and what a big boy he was deep down. "You will be afraid of me when you discover the truth, you little Sabine Sonnenschein."

As soon as they were back in Holland, they would be able to leave all this misery behind and, together with Sabine's mother, enter a double spring. He looked forward to the three of them driving through the bulb fields and enjoying the flowers. "I would like to leave my rags behind in the camp and right now lie down in a field with you."

While Sabine made an effort to keep Gebele interested and even agreed to an engagement, she also tried to talk him out of coming to Holland. But he was not to be dissuaded. "You will not put me off by painting your homeland in unattractive colors, my naughty Seelchen, and you are certainly not going to spoil the prospect of marriage by these means. No no, naughty little Seelchen."

Nothing could stop him from marrying Sabine. If only she would follow his wise advice about her foot, all would be well. She should think of the many women who lost their lives at the last moment because they could not keep up during an evacuation. That would be the worst possible thing that could happen to him. If Sabine died when rescue was within her grasp, "I can't think about it." So, however painful, she had to persevere.

Food was getting scarcer. The SS were now handing out only a sixth of the normal bread rations—perhaps an attempt at weakening the camp prisoners even more. Due to some thefts, Gebele had not sent Sabine any supplies for a few days, but he told her she could expect some more the next day, although she should meanwhile eat what was left over so far. Gebele suspected the food rations would shortly be even further reduced. "You have to keep eating to get well, then you can walk to the *Kommandantur* by yourself, while it is still allowed."

Since the last failed evacuation plans, Gebele hadn't mentioned any new evacuation projects, which must have weighted heavily on Sabine's mood. Freedom just got further away. Down below in the Wiener Graben, life was desolate. She did not even have a bed. But on the wall of the quarry opposite her barrack, she could see the spring blossom. A bottomless depression and desolation came over her. Every night there were bombardments nearby, and she wondered when it would be their turn.

In the Graben, rumors flew around about women being forced to have sex with each other, cannibalism, mass gassings and murders. Day and night there were constant fights over food, screaming and assaults. The fear and panic in the drafty, overcrowded huts must have been unbearable. The constant threats brought out the worst in everybody. It was survival of the fittest. No one cared for anyone else anymore. Just looking outside and seeing the men falling down the staircase weighted down by heavy rocks was an added torture.

Friday,
April 13, 1945

Gebele had received another letter via "our sweet female post lady" and by return sent Sabine a letter as well as clothes and a manicure set.

She had finally told Gebele some more details about her brothers. He looked forward to meeting them and was convinced they would get on well. "I especially feel some affinity with your youngest brother, although I don't know him. I imagine that I shall find in him a really good friend and brother-in-law." He wanted to know if they had hobbies other than sailing. "Do they like cars or play tennis?" Sabine would have to teach him sailing because "the Dutch are such water rats" and he didn't want to be inferior to them. But regarding other sports, such as gymnastics or parachuting, he was better than the average military man.

Sabine had started to write her life story for him, but had destroyed it. Gebele did not understand why. "If I had had the time you would definitely have had my life story in the form of a manuscript or even a short novel and you would then be able to gaze openly and without fearful trembling into my innermost soul and see what an evil human being I am."

He thought she might recoil at this, but then fall in love with him again. "Don't say I did not warn you. I am indeed a dreadful person and a thief, who has stolen your heart. Unfortunately my photo albums were destroyed by a bombardment, which is a shame because there were some nice photos of Scheveningen and Rotterdam in them."

Sabine was meanwhile worried about the ever shrinking bread rations for the prisoners. Gebele was too, but told her not to forget that "your big boy has enough reserves and access to further food reserves." He realized that Sabine was no doubt more worried for her friends and particularly for Hetty and Steijns, although Gebele thought she should stay happy and healthy and not worry about others, just himself. "I am very selfish, right?"

He was vague about the latest news from the Front. "Concerning news of our friends, I can only tell you that it is very positive, but there are no further details as there is an embargo throughout Germany regarding the war news. But I will talk to you about it in person."

Finally, at quarter past ten in the evening, he concluded this letter, which was one of the last ones she received from him:

I have to stop now in the hope and expectation that my angel will keep sending me her post daily via our courier and, if possible, also the dirty washing, which I will await with longing.

I also found a very short note with the letters that seemed to belong to this letter. A sort of cry of desperation:

Sabine! Please write to me. I am now writing to you.
Franz

Sunday,
April 15, 1945

In his letter of April 15, Gebele wondered with mounting disquiet why "meine liebe Sabine Sonnenschein" had not written to him. He was very upset and reminded her he had already written her two letters and had not received any in return. Why not? Was she angry with him? If so, why? Was something the matter? Was she sick? He was worried about her, but even more so for himself. His fear of losing her was immense and made him feel very insecure. But if she was just stalling him, he would take revenge the same way. She could count on that.

Had she actually received his letters, one from him and one from Dr. Steijns? And did she receive the items he had sent her, such as semolina, margarine, peas, bacon, bread, and something to file her nails, etc.? "I am especially curious if you have received two boxes and the sailing trousers."

For his own peace of mind, he accepted that her health had deteriorated and she had therefore not been able to make contact with him, neither by letter nor in person. He would investigate in the morning and leave his judgment until then.

It seemed Sabine's health had actually improved a little. Enough for her to leave her barrack and join workers in the field just outside the camp. Gebele had spotted her there working with the others.

The professor had told him the plaster cast would be removed the following day, and she must start practicing to walk. If all went well, she could join Gebele in his office at the end of the week, although he added, with what seemed like a little threat: "Of course I don't know if you want to work and cook with me, or if I may look after you in the future as I have done until now. I will have to wait for your reply and draw my conclusions accordingly."

The senior officers in the camp were by now making their escape plans in case the war suddenly ended, and Gebele had spent the last two days in the parking lot, testing all their cars for roadworthiness. Gebele too had put together an escape plan for Sabine and him. He wanted to see her to discuss it with her.

"Are you by chance able to drive? Or do you want to learn? I can lend you some books. You have time at the moment to study, just as I from my side and as per your wish, could refresh my French." He also reminded her that he was really keen to learn to sail, "when we get home."

He would have liked to take her on a tour of the world and travel for months, even on a honeymoon. As soon as he thought of marriage, he felt very happy and started fantasizing. It was these fantasies that had kept him going these last few weeks. "You know how stressed and worried I am, so bad I am hardly able to write to you."

Sabine at this stage was still in the Wiener Graben, where there was a plague of nits and lice. But Gebele assured her there was good news, although whether it was, was debatable.

The women who were able to work outside would be moved back into the camp itself and would be put in Barrack

19, situated at the edge of the main camp, the so-called slum. Surrounded on three sides by a high wall and fenced off with barbed wire from the rest of the camp, it was, according to Gebele, for a long time the scene of terrible suffering. People went there to be murdered or were left to die.

"But," he wrote, "it will be better for you here as the sanitation and hygiene are better than in the quarry." It was also quieter, and if there were any fights among the prisoners, then the camp guards were close by to restore order, unlike down below, where the prostitutes and Roma women were in charge and did as they liked with great cruelty.

But above all, she should stay optimistic and keep practicing using her ankle. If she could walk, she could come and work for him.

And now, to finish. I admit that I can no longer type, I am too dead tired to write anything else and I don't want to bother you with other things… In the hope that mein kleiner Sonnenschein will muster some sympathy for the emotional state of her sweet big boy and that at least some loving words from you will reach him (I so long for them).

I send you a thousand passionate kisses from the bottom of my heart.

Your dear big boy, Franz

Saturday,
April 21, 1945

Almost a week later, Gebele sent his last letter to Sabine. I don't know if there had been other letters in between or if she replied to his last one. But apparently they had managed to meet up.

Meine liebe kleine Sabine! Kleiner Sonnenschein!
A parting for both of us and certainly hard enough for me, but, at least I am at peace somewhat by knowing something of your complaint against me. Seelchen, I have told you the facts personally and on this basis I have no bad conscience. I have no mercy for schemers like Lisa and tricksters of that kind. If you choose to believe her comments rather than the solemn promises I have made to you, then I can only be saddened to the depths of my soul…

I give you my sacred word of honor—I don't think I overuse this term—when I reiterate by the lives of my mother and my dead child that I have never had anything to do with this female intriguer, not least and most especially because she is only seventeen. Is my word not enough for you? [...]

I have never been a villain or a cheat at any stage of my life. In this present case I regret only my good nature, which doesn't amount to much more than carelessness. But I take some comfort from my clear conscience and from what I must deduce from your behavior, namely that you really love me. That after all is worth more than the whole world to me and I am grateful to you, Seelchen, for it from the bottom of my heart. You will be rewarded for it constantly in the future and this I promise you on the death of my child and my mother.

I love you, Seelchen, and no other, more deeply than you can ever guess. Rest assured you can and may trust your big dear boy, who knows that trust is to be valued and respected. You may safely believe me that this situation renews the seal on my sacred pledge to you to visit you in your homeland as soon as we are free. For the moment I wish you on the occasion of your journey a speedy reunion with one thousand passionate kisses and with my best and heartfelt wishes.
Your big dear boy, Franz

Something had obviously happened to give Sabine a chance to create some distance between them.
A certain Lisa had been telling her things about Gebele that didn't tally with his own story. Perhaps she had had a relationship with Gebele or he had offered her food in return for sex, or perhaps even forced her to have sex with him. Whatever it was, Sabine no longer trusted Gebele. She would probably have had her suspicions regarding his good intentions and the tall stories he told about himself from the

beginning. No doubt he saved not only Sabine's life, but also that of Dr. Steijns and perhaps Hetty's and possibly others, but it is doubtful if he really was the Good Samaritan he made himself out to be in his letters to her.

Luckily, this upset did not affect her chances of an evacuation. This would be her last week in Mauthausen.

Free at Last

Ravensbrück was liberated by the Red Army on April 30, 1945. Mauthausen was officially liberated by the American and Canadian armies on May 5, 1945.

Two weeks earlier, on April 22, after weeks of intense expectation, speculation and frustration, suddenly, in the middle of the night, the female prisoners, including Sabine, were forced out of their barracks and onto the big Appellplatz for roll call. It was snowing and bitterly cold. Enormous fear took hold of the women. The gas chambers were still working at top capacity. Mass killings were still taking place on a daily basis. Even the day before liberation, 3,000 men were still sent to their death.

Dr. J. M. Rubli, a doctor from Zürich, described what happened that day. Rubli was the man in charge of the Red Cross transport that would take the women to safety:

Everyone thought they were going to be sent to the gas chambers. I walked between the rows and tried to reassure them that I was a Red Cross representative, but no one believed me. They had been lied to too many times.

Suddenly, in the first early daylight, I heard the distant roar of the engines. And saw the first buses appear from the woods and coming up the hill. Sixteen of my buses became visible through the gloom, one after the other, all painted white with a red cross. When they stopped the silence on the square was deafening and only when I ordered the drivers in French to get out of the buses an enormous cheering broke out. At last they could believe it was true.

The prisoners in the camp were now seeing kind, gentle, smiling, healthy-looking men full of concern for them. Helping them to get in the buses, asking how they felt. There were no words, only tears, lots of tears. The men told them to get into the buses as quickly as possible. The road situation changed by the hour due to the fighting and the Front moving continuously.

Sabine, her ankle still encased in plaster, managed to run back to her barrack and pick up the little suitcase Gebele had given her, containing his letters and a few clothes. She was not only still recovering from her broken ankle but also still very ill with pneumonia, jaundice and other injuries. It was only thanks to Gebele that she was still alive.

The camp commandant was ordered to give everyone some bread for the journey, but when he turned up with the usual moldy pieces, the Red Cross officer gave him short shrift, and he was forced to give out the bread meant for his guards. For the prisoners, this was an eye-opener, this all-powerful man being humiliated in front of all of them. He was puce with fury.

The series of convoys, consisting of 750 Dutch, Belgian, Norwegian, French and Italian women and including

sixty-seven men, was made up of the weakest, most sick
and wounded people. It was hoped they could survive this
difficult journey. Led by Dr. Rubli, the convoys took two
and a half days to reach the Swiss border, a distance of some
500 km.

The buses kept a distance between them to be less of a target from the air, and a small car drove ahead of each convoy
to make sure the road was clear, which often it was not. They
were forced to make a number of detours to avoid the fighting
and damaged roads. It was very risky as the Allies were carrying out bombing raids on convoys and, since it was known
that fleeing Germans also painted red crosses on their cars,
anything moving on the roads was a target. One bus ran out
of gas. Some got stuck in the snow. Miracles were performed
to keep the buses going.

When they stopped at nighttime, Dr. Rubli walked around
with his torch and asked everyone, *"Alles in Ordnung?"* Any
stomach pains, feeling ill? The women did not know what
to answer. It had been years since anyone asked them a question regarding their health. It was surreal. Suddenly there was
plenty of tea and food, although it was given sparingly to protect their stomachs. After years of starvation, they could not
cope with normal quantities of food. But above all, "the men
were so caring and worried about us," Sabine said.

At the German/Swiss border, there was a long delay. The
Swiss border control refused to let them through. They were
stuck there from five in the afternoon until 10 a.m. the following morning. The women had to spend the night on straw
mats in a hangar. Dr. Rubli spent all night going around giving everyone injections to keep them going. The Belgian girl
sleeping next to Sabine died in the night.

Once in Switzerland, Sabine and Hetty were taken to the
Kantonsspital (a hospital for infectious diseases) in Münsterlingen,

where they stayed for three months to recuperate. Still young, both Sabine and Hetty made a good recovery thanks to the excellent care and attention they received, not to mention the personal interest from the doctors.

On July 24, Hetty and Sabine were discharged from the hospital and allowed to go home. The journey was arranged via the Red Cross by Count Bernadotte. The train stopped in Brussels, where there was a large welcoming committee waiting for them. Many Belgian and Dutch flags were waved and national anthems played. A delicious meal was served. It was an emotional ceremony. Sabine later said, "We burst into tears if someone was nice to us."

However, on July 27, when they reached the Dutch border south of Eindhoven, the train was shunted into sidings. Many of the locals wanted to give them food and cigarettes, but it was forbidden by the authorities. It was feared the passengers carried infectious diseases and should therefore be quarantined in one of the Philips buildings in Eindhoven.

For Sabine and Hetty, who had spent three months in a Swiss hospital and were very clean, it was an unnecessary measure. Sabine even said later, "We were cleaner than the Dutch." It felt as though they were back in the camp, sleeping on straw on the floor. There were no showers, although they could wash themselves in halls, where men freely walked around while the women were naked. They were still not truly free.

A Dutch person who came to look for a friend, but who recognized Sabine, managed to get her and Hetty out of the quarantine. They spent the night at his house and then traveled to The Hague the following day. Hetty was reunited with an aunt, but Sabine spent some time searching for her mother, who was eventually found to be living in a small attic room. Sabine was the first of her three children to return home.

Moeder Bien had desperately tried to visit her daughter
when she heard she was alive and in a Swiss hospital, but she
could not get permission to travel. Her Red Cross colleagues
wrote her a kind letter to say how happy they were to hear
of Sabine's homecoming and wished them both all the best.

Dr. Steijns had also returned home safely and had resumed
his practice when he sent Sabine a note to thank her once
again:

Dear child,
It is possible that you were happy to hear I arrived safely
back in Holland, but you cannot have been as happy as
I was with your postcard. How grateful I am to you I
shall never forget and the fact I can write this is for a
large part due to the help Gebele gave me, which is entirely thanks to your instigation. I hope to convey this
to you in person soon.

Dr. Steijns also asked after Hetty and wanted to know if
Sabine had received the long letter from Gebele that he smuggled out of the camp and sent on to her.

I forwarded it immediately after my arrival in Switzerland.
A firm handshake. Steijns

The letter that Gebele wrote after Sabine had left the camp
and asked Dr. Steijns to post to her was not in the archives, so
I suspect she never received it.

I did find another surprising letter, though, sent to her by a
Dr. Laurent who had treated her in Münsterlingen. He wrote
to confess that he missed her and Hetty's cheerful company.
"Since you left I feel as though someone has died." He also

admitted that he was in love, "probably with you." It is quite clear from the rest of the letter that this is the case. He also apologized for not coming to say his goodbyes when the train left. He had found it too painful. But while he would have loved to see her again, he felt that due to his poor pay and prospects, he could not offer her any future.

All over Holland, trains from the camps began to return with the survivors. Sabine said, "We all went to the station for every train to welcome them back. There were so many tears, with happiness to see old friends again, but also tears to hear the sad news of the many who had perished and were not coming back."

Home

Gebele

After many years in camps, Gebele himself must have been traumatized by his surroundings and everything that had happened to him and what he had witnessed.

But what sort of a person was he in the camp? Did he treat prisoners badly, or did he, as he claimed, try and do his best for them? It is difficult to judge him, considering these were such extraordinary times and circumstances. His style of writing to our eyes is very stiff and old-fashioned, but so passionate. This sudden intense love revived a desperate and lonely man, dead in his emotions, who suddenly, in the midst of this daily hell, found a reason to look forward to the future again due to a chance encounter with Sabine.

There are strange contradictions in his character. The fact that he was so appalled at Dr. Steijns's appearance is surprising and gives the impression that perhaps he had not seen prisoners as human beings until then. Had he not noticed there were thousands of men and women in the same condition?

Perhaps meeting Sabine suddenly opened his eyes to what was really going on?

Initially I read that Gebele was executed a few days after Sabine left, but some digging in the Munich archives with the help of the Mauthausen archivist revealed that he actually went home to Munich, where he died on September 19, 1945, due to circulatory collapse during an operation.

He had obviously been an unwell man for some time, not surprising considering the conditions in the camp. The awfulness of his surroundings must have affected him mentally too. It is clear from his letters that he veered between wild optimism and deep depression. Life after the camps in the normal world would have been very difficult for him. There is no mention anywhere of what happened to his family. Did they keep in touch while he was in the camp? Did he find any of them after returning home? Did he try and contact Sabine through the papers?

His profession is sometimes given as a mechanic, in other documents as clockmaker. Were his stories of being a pilot true or made up? He himself related that his diploma of engineering was rescinded, but gave only a vague explanation why, and it is unclear what he may have lied about. Only one thing seems sure: he was a *Berufsverbrecher*, a career criminal. He claimed his father was a liqueur manufacturer, but according to official documents, he was variously described as a coachman and a mineral water manufacturer.

Just as I was finishing the manuscript for this book, I suddenly received a reply from the Arolsen Archives to my question asked more than a year before. The papers confirmed he had undergone several operations, some as part of research, including one for a trial of a typhoid vaccine.

His marital state showed he was divorced, and to my amazement, under children it said two.

The *Staatsarchiv* München also revealed that his wife, Emma Gebele, whom he had claimed to have shot dead, was still very much alive in 1978. Perhaps he did not actually shoot her dead as he had claimed, or perhaps she was his second wife. This would explain his short sentence of three months. His divorce date is unclear, either 1934 or 1941.

The Arolsen papers also showed that Franz Josef Gebele was imprisoned in Mauthausen on May 12, 1941, by the *Kripo* (criminal police) in Munich. He claimed to have been imprisoned for eleven years. So, where was he before 1941? In Dachau, which was a criminal jail before the war? There don't seem to be any records about his time before the war.

Sabine herself never mentioned Gebele to me or anyone else as far as I know, until she was interviewed for a book by Dunya Breur and sometime later by my daughter for a work project about the war. To them she mentioned that he had saved her life, but that everything he had told her was nothing but lies. But what were these lies? About his family? His qualifications? His love for her or her love for him?

The first time I came across him was when I found a note in my mother's archive attached to his letters. On it was also his home address: Victoriastraße 21–23, Munich.

So many questions to which I have not found any answers.

Whatever the truth, I cannot deny that he did save her life, and also Hetty's and Dr. Steijns's and perhaps others'. That is certainly something to be grateful for.

Moeder Bien
and Sabine

Moeder Bien was in dire straits after the war. She had lost her house and most of her possessions. What had not been destroyed by the bombardments she had put into storage, due to constantly having to move house. When she came to collect her belongings after the war, she found all of them had been sold to the Germans by the storage depot. Her prewar pension, which had just about kept her going previously, had now dwindled to nothing.

Sabine returned home from the war in poor health and traumatized. Her fiancé, Taro Roeper-Bosch, had been shot down in his Spitfire at the beginning of the war, most of her friends had perished, and many of those who survived had emigrated. Her two brothers, having spent years in Japanese concentration camps, were also in poor health and traumatized. They had barely survived the camps.

Moeder Bien had been alone during the war, not knowing what had happened to her children. So many of Sabine's friends were lost: Taro Roeper-Bosch, Gerard Vinkesteijn, Dr.

Krediet, Broer Moonen, Jan van den Hoek and many more. The suffering in the aftermath of the war for those who had been in the Resistance and had survived is hard to describe. All the lives of often young people were brutally ended by execution or fighting or being sent to concentration camps.

However, Sabine had to start her life anew. But where to begin? She had no accommodation, furniture, clothes or any possessions left. Only her mother and a few close girlfriends. Her first task was to find a job and earn some money. During a party at Villa Maarheeze in Wassenaar, a suburb of The Hague where the Bureau of National Intelligence was housed, she was invited to join the Secret Service. She began her training straightaway by learning codes. I found instructions and samples of her "homework" practicing codes in her archive. But she soon decided that this was not a job for her. I can understand that she could not handle any more secrecy and stress at this stage. Being a spy did not appeal to her.

For a short time, she became engaged in November 1945 to Leslie Chater, a handsome English lieutenant colonel. He was attached to the Canadian army that had liberated Holland and was involved in negotiations about the German capitulation. After the war he interrogated German Nazis in Holland, in particular in Camp Amersfoort. The mystery of how my mother came to be in possession of the papers relating to the tribunal of the three guards and her interrogation was finally solved. Leslie had found them in the Amersfoort archives and had passed them on to Sabine. The engagement did not last long. Sabine had not recovered emotionally or physically from her experiences. She probably also did not want to move to another country at this stage and leave her mother and friends behind again. Getting used to normal life was hard enough.

For years she suffered nightmares. She had seen and experienced such horrors for so long, and at nighttime she could not avoid reliving them. She had permanent trouble with her digestion due to long-term starvation and became obsessed with food. No crumb was ever allowed to be thrown away or wasted.

She found it difficult to pick up the threads of normal life again and, like many other survivors, suffered from a profound sense of sadness and probably guilt that she had survived when so many of her friends had not. After the war, the emotional dam broke.

She herself said, "These memories are so awful. I managed to hide them from myself for a long time, but after the war, when normal life resumed, they kept resurfacing, and I began to understand what I had endured and survived, which created shock waves and abnormal reactions in me for a long time."

In a questionnaire called "Women in the Resistance 1940–45," her verdict on herself was down-to-earth, though: "I did nothing special, I just helped where I could."

Peter

Queen Wilhelmina returned to the already liberated part of the south of Holland to a village near Breda on May 2, 1945, almost five years to the day after German occupation. The plane carrying her home contained just five people: the queen herself, Princess Juliana, a government official, and Peter Tazelaar and Erik Hazelhoff Roelfzema as her appointed adjudants. She settled for the time being at the Anneville Estate in Ulvenhout, near Breda. This would be her temporary residence until the whole of Holland was liberated.

The end of the war was expected any day, and when it happened, on May 4, Peter was having a drink with some military police on guard at the gates. They were listening to music on the radio, when suddenly, it was interrupted by a special announcement. The German High Command had capitulated in Holland. The war had ended.

Peter was so excited by this fantastic news that he forgot all protocol and raced to the queen's study, bursting in unannounced and barely able to speak from emotion. He was the first person to inform the queen that hostilities had ended. The queen, equally overcome, shook his hand endlessly and gave him two big kisses on his cheeks.

Although Peter was now formally in service to the queen as her adjutant, court life was intolerable for him and thus short-lived. He could not live a life restricted by rules and regulations. Queen Wilhelmina understood him only too well. She had a soft spot for Peter and allowed him more leeway than anybody else, but there was a limit to the freedom he was given. Peter resigned within months, but the special place she kept in her heart for him was such that, five years after her death, Peter, at her request, would lay the wreath at her grave on behalf of all *Engelandvaarders*. Even when she was no longer alive, she still honored him.

In the beginning of August 1945, Peter flew out to Ceylon and from there on to Java, not only with the intention of collecting his mother from a Japanese concentration camp, but also to fight the Japanese. But the war in the East had ended abruptly after the Americans dropped the atom bombs on Hiroshima and Nagasaki on August 6 and 9, and the Japanese, as a result, had capitulated immediately. So when Peter arrived in the Dutch East Indies, he joined the Military Police of the First Infantry Battalion of the Royal Dutch Indonesian Army (KNIL) as its head instead.

Indonesia, or the Dutch East Indies, had been part of the Dutch empire for nearly three hundred years, until in the early twentieth century the fight for decolonization slowly began. When the Japanese invaded Indonesia in 1940, many of the freedom fighters were supportive as they initially saw the Japanese as liberators from the Dutch. But they soon realized that they would be exchanging one yoke for another. When the war in the East suddenly ended with the dropping of the atom bombs, these freedom fighters turned on the

Dutch still remaining as well as on some of their own population, such as the Chinese and the communists. The atrocities they committed on their own countrymen were terrible. Peter was in charge of tracking down and interrogating these fighters. It was a difficult job for him, because many of these men had been his friends from his youth. But he could not tolerate their cruel behavior, which caused him a great deal of shock and heartache. In March 1946, he was wounded and returned to Holland.

Peter and Sabine

Not long after the war, Sabine and Peter reunited. During an RAF party in The Hague, Peter met up again with Lon Versteijnen, a friend of both Peter and Sabine. Lon had been in the Resistance and was in Ravensbrück at the same time as Sabine. Peter wanted to know if Sabine was still alive, and Lon supplied him with her address. He soon paid her a visit, and in the general party atmosphere and sense of enormous relief that better times were ahead, they made a hasty and in retrospect unwise decision, like many others, to get married. At that stage after their war experiences, neither was emotionally able to live a normal everyday life. There was still a lot of hardship and unrest for everybody, not least for those who had suffered so much. Professional help to deal with trauma was not really available in those days.

After their marriage in December 1946, Sabine got pregnant almost immediately, and Peter's job at the KLM Royal Dutch Airline as an operations manager offered them a chance to escape the aftermath of the war and go to India for a few years. But shortly before their departure, Sabine became very unwell, losing weight rapidly, going down to 48 kg. She still could hardly tolerate any food as a result of her previous starvation diet. Peter flew out to Karachi ahead of Sabine, who stayed behind until after my birth, leaving her feeling very miserable and lonely.

Dr. Steijns provided a safe haven for her. He and his wife were eternally grateful to her and had offered to deliver any babies she might have in the future. They had resumed their practice again after having reclaimed their home from the Germans who had commandeered it during the war. To their joy, they found their family silver and their daughter's dolls back in the garden where they had buried them. Both I and my brother a few years later were born in this clinic with the help of Dr. Steijns. After all she had suffered while in the *Revier*, particularly in Ravensbrück, it was a great luxury for Sabine to get such personal care and attention from people who cared for her. She would have felt very sad, however, that Peter was not with her but in India.

Before flying out to India, my mother and I spent a month in a one-bedroom apartment in Amsterdam. Unfortunately, 1947 was one of the coldest winters on record, and she told me later that she had to hand-wash her clothes and my cotton nappies in cold water and dry them around the stove, so it was a miserable time for her. Then, when I was six weeks old, we flew out to join Peter.

Of course, I don't remember this period, and apart from a few tiny photos, I don't really know what life was like there for them. Occasionally we flew back to Holland for a few weeks' respite from the heat, which probably did not suit Sabine's health very well, and stayed with friends in the Catshuis in The Hague. This beautiful house stands on the Sorghvliet Estate and dates from the 1600s. In the war, the German spy training school, the "Agentenschule West," was based there. According to my mother, I learned to walk during one of our visits there. Since 1963, the Catshuis has been the official residence of the prime minister, and various ministers have actually lived there with their families.

Altogether we spent two years in India, in Karachi and Kolkata, but eventually it was time to go home. My mother and I flew back ahead, and while searching for a flat to rent, Mrs. Roeper-Bosch, Taro's mother, kindly offered us the loan of Taro's old bedroom, installing a heater and furniture to make it comfortable. We found a first-floor flat near her in Scheveningen and lived there for two years before moving to another flat, also in The Hague. My brother was born while we lived there.

Peter could not settle down, though. Working in an office for the KLM did not suit him, nor did everyday family life. He was too much of a free spirit, restless and looking for challenges. In 1950, he left the KLM and started working for Shell. He had already started doing undercover work, and this new job gave him the opportunity of traveling, which provided a cover for his spying activities as a secret agent. At first he worked for the Dutch Secret Service, but later for the CIA. His very dangerous missions behind the Iron Curtain meant he often disappeared for weeks or months on end, leaving Sabine on her own and in the dark as to where he was, as well as in financial difficulties. He would disappear suddenly and reappear equally suddenly sometime later.

In the mid-1950s, Shell offered him the opportunity to work in Curaçao, which he decided to accept, but the marriage had hit rock bottom, and my mother refused to go with him. She was still ill and painfully thin. They divorced in 1955.

Sabine

Another difficult period started for Sabine. Divorced single women in the 1950s were regarded as second-class citizens, and with no money and two small children, these were lonely times. Around my eighth birthday, my mother received an invitation from a Dutch friend to come to Ibiza. It was then a relatively unknown island, visited mainly by a few artists, film stars, Mafia members in hiding, and people who sought an alternative lifestyle. There was no airport either there or on Mallorca, and the only way to reach the islands was by boat from Barcelona, an overnight trip.

We rented a small house and quickly made many friends of all nationalities. Life on Ibiza suited us so well that Sabine had thoughts of settling there permanently. My brother and I were very happy joining in the many trips around both Ibiza and Formentera, having picnics and barbecues on deserted beaches and searching for crabs on the rocks below our house.

But after a few months, I suddenly became very ill. The only (Spanish) "doctor" on the island had only spent a few years working in a hospital in Barcelona as a medical orderly. He gave me painkillers and promised he would come by in another week. He was on holiday in the meantime. But I deteriorated, and my mother became very worried. Our German neighbor, also a young woman recently divorced with two small children, had also come to Ibiza to recover from her divorce. To her dismay, the first person she met on the island was her ex-husband, who had also come for a holiday, with a colleague. Both the men were well-known urologists in Germany. Overcoming her reluctance, she asked them for help for me.

By that time, I was seriously ill with a kidney infection, and they insisted I should go to the hospital. But there was no hospital. The trip by boat to Barcelona would be too long and dangerous, and in any case ran only once a week. So, after some arm wrestling with the local pharmacy (as foreign doctors they were not allowed to prescribe medication), they managed to obtain some medicines and for a week came and gave me very painful injections twice a day. They were very charmed by my mother, and after I got better, they took her out a few times. How ironic that ten years after the war, my life was saved by two German doctors.

After this episode, however, my mother decided that the island was not a suitable place to bring up children. This was reinforced by the very poor education available there. To my brother's and my intense disappointment, we left paradise and returned to Holland. I have never seen my mother so happy and carefree again since that time. Her "party girl" side came out again for a short while.

Despite having many boyfriends in the following years, she never wanted to share her life with any of them until she met Jan Blank in her mid-fifties. Their marriage lasted until his death (in 1998) twenty-three years later.

In 2009, while traveling around India for work, I received an urgent message from my brother. Our mother, by now in a care home, was suddenly deteriorating rapidly. I was only in my first week of a seven-week trip, and I had many appointments to fulfill in Varanasi, Kolkata, Kalimpong and Darjeeling. What to do? She had had these episodes before and had recovered. Peter advised me to wait and see. He would inform me every day whether her condition was stable or getting worse. After a few weeks, once I got to Darjeeling, an urgent message came to return home as soon as possible. It was a question of possibly hours now.

My hotel was owned by a very sweet Tibetan couple whom I had gotten to know well during my many visits with them. When I told them the reason for my sudden departure, they immediately offered to go to their local monastery and ask the monks to say *puja* (prayers) for my mother. Hours later, after having rebooked my train and flight and while packing my suitcase, I received another message from Peter. I was prepared for the worst, but instead was told that our mother had made a miraculous recovery and had been found wandering through the home's corridors by the carers. When I told my Tibetan friends, they were delighted, but did not seem surprised. They told me that that afternoon, several hundred monks had indeed said *puja* for her, and they assured me this was the power of prayer. Since then, whenever I tell this story, many others also assure me of this power of prayer.

It may be so, but I think it was also my mother's own strong will to live that played a role. She told me years before that as long as she kept walking, she could not die. When she started living in the care home, she did always walk along the corridors, endlessly. She was by no means a walker at any other time in her life, but perhaps towards the end of her life, the memories of those who fell or lay down during her time in the camps came back again.

Sabine recovered well and lived for another three years. She died fourteen years after the death of her second husband, in 2012.

I inherited her life story.

Last But Not Least

Little did I know what a journey the story of my mother's life would turn out to be. When I first opened the large boxes some years after her death, they appeared to contain lots of old documents, quite a few in German, and many letters, but also enclosed were some fascinating photos of student balls, sailing parties, and Taro's regiment practicing and presumably preparing for war. A photographic story in itself of Sabine's prewar and beginning of the wartime. I saw a happy young woman who had no idea what life had in store for her.

The most intriguing finds, though, were the two large bundles of letters, each held together by pieces of string. One beautifully and elegantly handwritten in German, but unreadable for me, and the second one love letters from Taro. When I eventually read his letters, I really understood what importance he had played in her life. Her first and most important love of her life.

In order to try and understand more of the information I found, my brother Peter and I decided to visit first Amersfoort and then Ravensbrück. Both are of course unrecognizable today compared with how they looked during the war.

In Ravensbrück, we were lucky with our very knowledgeable guide, Matthias Heyl, who for several hours took us on a private guided tour, including to the Siemens site, and gave endless explanations, even producing the transport list of my mother's arrival in the camp and remarking that it would have been her one hundredth birthday a few days later. We were quite moved by the personal attention they gave to our visit.

Six months later, I also visited Mauthausen and again found a very kind guide waiting to take me round. I expressed surprise that a young man like himself would be so interested in working in a place with such a grim history. He told me his grandfather had been in the SS but had never spoken of it, and he was trying to come to terms with this and understand his own family's history.

Both guides spent a long time showing me around the camps, or what was left of them, and answering all our questions. I am very grateful to them for their personal attention.

The German letters were at that time not yet translated, and I had no idea what was in them, but when I showed them to the archivist in the office in Mauthausen, he was very interested.

It took nearly two years to find someone who could not only translate them, as they were written in old-fashioned German, but also decipher the handwriting.

Eventually I was lucky to be introduced to Richard (and his partner, Irene). Richard has done an amazing job in not only just translating the letters but also reproducing the sense of sometimes exaggerated formality and the feel of the era. I am very grateful for his enthusiasm, his interest, his knowledge and the advice he gave during this rather long process.

While the translating was proceeding, I contacted the

Arolsen Archives, the international tracing service, and the International Center on Nazi Persecution to try and find out more about Gebele or indeed if there were still any living relatives. They have been very helpful in supplying me with information on him, but no relatives have so far been found. They are still looking, though.

Andreas Kranebitter, from the Mauthausen archives in Vienna, also was kind enough to offer assistance and wrote to the Munich archives, which supplied yet more bits of information about Gebele. Some of it conflicted with what Gebele had told Sabine.

My mother spoke very little about the conditions in the camps or what happened to her, other than to say she was always very hungry and cold. She did write quite a few reports after the war, but mostly factual, *i.e.*, dates, people in the camp with her, etc., but also some details relating to incidents that had happened. They were of course very useful for my research, but did not give me a clear picture of everyday life in the camps.

My information about everyday camp life therefore comes from other sources.

Dunya Breur, whose mother Aat was in Ravensbrück with Sabine (and who drew the portrait of her, now in the Rijksmuseum along with all her other drawings made in the camp), came to see my mother when she wrote her book *Een Verborgen Herinnering*. I recognized some descriptions in her book from Sabine's reports, and Dunya quotes Sabine several times in her book as well. I have therefore used some of her descriptions in my book as I feel many came from Sabine herself.

Further sources came from the internet, other people's stories and witness reports, various books, and archives, in particular those of the NIOD in Amsterdam and the National Archives in The Hague. Sarah Helm's book, *If This Is a*

Woman, especially provided detailed information and is a true encyclopedia of the history and life of Ravensbrück.

The museums in both Ravensbrück and Mauthausen also provided much information.

The conditions in the camps changed continuously, especially towards the end of the war. Chaos reigned. Camp authorities desperately tried, on the one hand, to destroy all administrative evidence of what had gone on and send record numbers of women to their deaths while trying to clear the camp; and on the other hand, they tried to improve conditions within the camp, particularly the *Revier* so that they could show the Allies how well they had looked after their prisoners. Conditions are therefore described differently by different people at different times.

A great deal of the information on Peter Tazelaar, my father, comes from Victor Laurentius, who has been endlessly helpful regarding research and supplying information. He has written his own biography on Peter—*De Grote Tazelaar*. His help and advice with this book have been invaluable.

Soldier of Orange, written by Erik Hazelhoff Roelfzema, which has been made into a film and musical, also provided a useful and fascinating insight into his and Peter's time in London and their adventures during the war.

Regarding the betrayal by Sabine's boss, I researched the National and Central Archives in The Hague. Because of the possibility of any of his relatives still living, I have chosen not to reveal his name or the file numbers in the archives.

I have donated the papers about the interrogation in Amersfoort in connection with Sabine's stay, and the upset this caused, to Camp Amersfoort.

Sabine's personal archive, including the original text of the German letters in full, is now in the Resistance Museum in Amsterdam and also available to view on their website.

When I first started writing this story, I came across a TV interview with Selma van de Perre, who had just written a book about her time in Ravensbrück. She was there at the same time as my mother, and she mentioned several women whom I recognized as her friends too. So, intrigued, I contacted the publishers to ask if they could put me in touch with Selma so that I could find out if she and Sabine might have known each other. And indeed, Selma had known my mother.

I am very grateful to Catharina Schilder, Selma's editor, who replied to my request, for not only putting me in touch with Selma but also expressing an interest in my book, which at that time was only a story to pass on to my children.

She also arranged for it to be translated from English into Dutch, my Dutch after living more than fifty years in England being rather rusty.

Bert Natter not only has been an amazing translator but also became involved in some of the research and has been a source of encouragement and knowledge and a shoulder to lean on.

And Finally

A small but rather amazing incident happened just before finishing this book.

While out on a day trip to Liverpool with friends, we decided to have a rest in a local park and sit in the sunshine. As we walked towards a bench, my eye fell, in passing, on a memorial stone engraved "611 Squadron." It nagged me that it sounded familiar, but I could not immediately think why.

On returning to the memorial, I realized it was the name of Taro's squadron that he flew with when he was shot down. And indeed, there on the memorial plaque was his name inscribed along with the other pilots who had lost their lives. The memorial was only placed there in 2019.

What a coincidence. To find his name, nearly eighty years later in a public park in England, near my home. It was just meant to be: a small connection with the past and a fitting end to his part in this story.

★ ★ ★ ★ ★

Bibliography

Sources

Archives in the musea of Camps Ravensbrück and Mauthausen, via Matthias Heyl and Andreas Kranebitter.

Arolsen Archives—International Center on Nazi Persecution.

Letters, documents and reports from the private archive of Sabine Zuur, including:

83 letters from Taro Roeper Bosch, written between September 1938–May 10, 1940.

17 letters from Franz Josef Gebele, written in March and April 1945.

Report for the Red Cross, written in 1947.

Report for the Stichting 1940–1945, written in 1962.

Telephone interview by Karen Taylor, my daughter, with her *Oma* Sabine Blank Zuur in 1995 for a project on the fifty-year commemoration of the liberation.

NIOD Institute for War, Holocaust and Genocide Studies. With thanks to Hubert Berkhout.

Biographies

Berendsen, Anne, 1946. Vrouwen kamp Ravensbrück. Utrecht: W. de Haan NV.

Breur, Dunya, 1983/1995. Een verborgen herinnering. Drawings from Ravensbrück by Aat Breur-Hibma. Nijmegen: SUN.

Laurentius, Victor, 2009/2010. De grote Tazelaar, Ridder en Rebel. The Hague: Foundation: Peter Tazelaar.

Hazelhoff Roelfzema, Erik, 1971. Soldaat van Oranje 40–45. Graven-hage: Stok.

Helm, Sarah, 2015. If this is a woman. Inside Ravensbrück: Hitler's concentration camp for women. London: Little, Brown.

Staatsarchiv München.

With regard to the betrayal of "boss Piet," I consulted his files in the National Archive and the Centraal Archief Bijzondere Rechtspleging (CABR). In order to protect any possible descendants, I have chosen not to reveal his name or his file numbers.

The documents that describe the events of October 10–12, 1943, and the resulting interrogations have been donated, on my mother's behalf, to the Stichting Nationaal Monument Kamp Amersfoort, where they can be inspected by interested parties.

Historian Richard Hoving, author of Josef Kotalla's biography *De beul van Amersfoort*, supplied additional information regarding this episode.

The quotes by Sabine Zuur about the journey from Ravensbrück to Mauthausen on pages 101–103 are taken from Dunya Breur's book *Een verborgen herinnering.*

As is the quote from Sabine Zuur about her arrival in Mauthausen on pages 107–108 and the report about the bombing of Amstetten on pages 110–112.

The report by Dr. Rubli regarding the Red Cross transport of which Sabine was a part of, on pages 175–176, was made to the International Committee of the Red Cross, available in archives.

The letters by Franz Josef Gebele can be viewed at
www.verzetsmuseum.org/nl/kennisbank/sabine-zuur.